Security Consulting, Second Edition

Security Consulting
Second Edition

Charles A. Sennewald, CMC, CPP, CPO

Butterworth–Heinemann

Boston   Oxford   Melbourne   Singapore   Toronto   Munich   New Delhi   Tokyo

∞ Recognizing the importance of preserving what has been written, Butterworth–Heinemann prints its books on acid-free paper whenever possible.

Library of Congress Cataloging-in-Publication Data
Sennewald, Charles A., 1931–
    Security consulting / Charles A. Sennewald.—2nd ed.
        p.   cm.
    Includes bibliographical references and index.
    ISBN 0-7506-9643-5 (pbk.: alk. paper)
    1. Security consultants—Handbooks, manuals, etc.
I. Title.
HV8290.S47   1995
363.2'89'068—dc20   95-19952
                                                                                      CIP

British Library Cataloguing-in-Publication Data
A catalogue record for this book is available from the British Library.

The publisher offers discounts on bulk orders of this book.
For information, please write:

Manager of Special Sales
Butterworth–Heinemann
313 Washington Street
Newton, MA 02158-1626

10 9 8 7 6 5 4 3 2

Printed in the United States of America

Thank God, from whom all blessings flow.

Contents

Preface

Security consulting had flourished by the mid-1980s as an integral, necessary discipline within the security industry. Professionals engaging in consulting prior to the 1980s were few and far between. Notable among this group were such pioneers as Timothy Walsh, Philip Schiedermayer, Don Darling, Bob Curtis, Thad Weber, David Berger, Roy Wesley, and Steve Carlson.

The practice of consulting came of age in 1984 through the founding of its own professional organization, the International Association of Professional Security Consultants (IAPSC). That organization, in addition to creating a forum for communication among consultants, defined consulting, set certain standards, and developed a professional code of ethics. The principles of a speech I delivered at that organization's first meeting still apply:

I hold the minutes of a meeting held at the Waldorf-Astoria in New York on September 20, 1972. The heading reads: First Organizational Meeting of Professional Protection Consultants.

In attendance were nine practicing consultants. They developed a constitution and came up with a name: the American Academy of Protection Consultants. They had expectations, but for whatever reasons, the Academy didn't fly. The time just wasn't right.

But the time now *is* right. We are regathered here, and we too have expectations, and we are already airborne. And we will grow. As the security industry continues in maturation and sophistication, so will the needs grow for professional guidance and counseling.

Let me take a look down the road, to focus on two long-range goals and one new opportunity.

The first goal is to reshape the image and reputation of the *security consultant*. We must take positive steps to legitimize that term and discourage abuse of that title by anybody who merely wants to call themselves a security consultant without earning the title.

The second goal is to create a better understanding among ourselves as to our real role as consultants. One of our problems, believe it or not, is in that very title: security consultant. Why? Too much emphasis is placed on the word *security*.

It should go without saying that we have expertise in the security field. But our orientation should be as professional consultants; we should be consultants first, and security experts second. How many have hung out their security consultant's shingle, only to fail? Many failures could be attributed to a lack of consulting skills, not a deficiency in security knowledge.

Another opportunity exists in forensic consulting, which includes expert eyewitness testimony. There's a growing demand for security experts to assess the adequacy or inadequacy of security in a given setting and subsequently provide testimonial support for that assessment. No one other than a qualified expert is permitted the privilege of expressing an opinion in our judicial system.

And so, the time for the security consultant finally has come. We are few, but we are of good quality and we follow the highest standards. To live up to our worthy goals and new opportunities, we must at all times be responsible professionals.

I'm proud to be a part of this new consulting field. To those who have played a role in making this a reality, we are all grateful. And to those who join us for the first time, who are new to this exciting profession of consulting, I welcome you.

So this simple handbook is a compilation of ideas, strategies, and practical advice reflecting the thinking of my colleagues as well as myself. Put another way, I'm a better consultant today through my association with my professional peers, and I pass along their contributions to you.

I have been asked, "Aren't you concerned about overcrowding the consulting business by welcoming newcomers and sharing ideas that could lead to their success, and more competition?" My answer is, "On the contrary, I welcome qualified new colleagues who will enhance our profession."

This book is meant not only to offer insight into methods and procedures for successful consulting, but also to infuse this exciting new field with its own sense of identity as well as standards for professionalism.

Chuck Sennewald
San Diego County, California

Acknowledgments

I am truly grateful to friends and peers who always rose to my call for their input. To name each one puts me in the same position as the pastor who annually wishes to thank all those who have helped. His list includes the choir, organist, ushers, ladies of the altar guild, etc.; and invariably he overlooks someone, every year!

Those who most actively assisted me in the original edition of this work included Jack Janson, Jr., Huntington Beach, CA; David Berger, Los Angeles, CA; James Broder, Walnut Creek, CA; Robert Murphy, Notre Dame, IN; and David Kent, New Orleans, LA.

Other consultants who contributed in some measure include Robert Gallati, Punta Gorda, FL; Steven Keller, Deltona, FL; Gerald O'Rourke, New York, NY; Tony Potter, Atlanta, GA; Robert Shellow, Bethesda, MD; Ira Somerson, Plymouth Meeting, PA; Ray Chambers, Largo, FL; John Laye, Moraga, CA; Scott Roulston, Cleveland, OH; Mark Warrington, Portland, OR; and James Ryan, Petersburg, VA.

Those consultants who so generously assisted me in this second edition are: John "Jack" Case, Del Mar, CA; Mark Warrington, Portland, OR; Ira Somerson, Plymouth Meeting, PA; David Berger, Los Angeles, CA; Gerald O'Rourke, New York, NY; Ray Chambers, Largo, FL; William "Bill" Wilson, Lake Elsinore, CA; Kevin Murray, Clinton, NJ; Steve Kaufer, Palm Springs, CA; Tom Roemer, Buffalo Grove, IL; John Smith, Natick, MA; Robert Spiel, Chicago, IL; and Ed Clendenin, Houston, TX.

That is not to say others have not helped in some way. Half the members of the International Association of Professional Security Consultants have made some form of contribution if only by example. I have been greatly impressed with the array of those consultants' philosophy, style, methodology, and entrepreneurial creativity. The ranks of consultants comprise very different characters and personalities that have inspired me to write about this profession. I have been privileged to rub elbows with this diverse collection of professionals.

I must acknowledge Laurel DeWolf, Associate Editor of Butterworth–Heinemann, for her encouragement to pursue this second edition.

And lastly I acknowledge my life partner Connie, widely known to friends and relatives as "Precious," for support in all I do. I couldn't have made it without her.

Introduction

There are really three types or categories of security consultants:

- Security Management Consultants whose principal focus is in the classic managerial arena such as organizational design, budgeting, policy development and procedural development ... in our case, as it pertains to security, loss prevention, and protection of assets strategies.
- Security Technical or Engineering Consultants whose expertise lies, obviously, in the technical arena, i.e., technical specifications, designing systems, specifying equipment and hardware, etc. ... all to augment, enhance, or otherwise facilitate the security of a given building or facility.
- Forensic Security Consultants are those management and technical consultants who direct their energy and talents in litigation-oriented assignments, i.e., analyzing the evidence discovered in lawsuits with the intention of determining liability or not and serving, if appropriate, as expert witnesses in our state and federal courts of law.

This book addresses the practice of consulting in the management and forensic disciplines. That's not to suggest engineering consultants don't have the same professional problems as the rest of us, indeed I know they do, but I write from an experiential base that is not technical and hence I lack the necessary qualifications to address their particular concerns. However, there is information contained herein that could be helpful.

Chapter 1

Security Consulting as a Profession

The growth of security management consulting as a profession parallels that of the entire industry of protection in the private sector, whose products and services have dramatically expanded in the last decade and a half. The increasing demand for consulting services comes as no surprise with all the corporate down-sizing, out-sourcing, and technological advances. What does come as a surprise is how few security practitioners have recognized the opportunities it presents.

Security consulting offers the most exciting new career opportunity within our industry. Indeed, it represents the freshest and most rewarding new career path since security management. Time was when senior positions represented the "hot button" in the protection industry. Those executive posts are still highly desirable, but now another challenging alternative—consulting as a profession—has come of age.

COMPARISON OF THE SECURITY EXECUTIVE AND THE CONSULTANT

As a full-time, salaried employee, the *security executive* of a given corporation serves in some measure as a proprietary or in-house consultant to senior-level management. He or she recommends appropriate and cost-effective strategies to achieve a wide variety of security objectives, loss control, crime prevention, and investigative goals. Certainly a rewarding dimension of that work is the chance to manage and oversee the implementation of the plan and experience the success of the strategy. That is no small reward. Additionally, the company security executive enjoys many employee benefits, including job security.

The *security consultant*, as an independent operator, gives up such job security and company-provided benefits. More often than not the consultant has little to do with the organizational activity of the company and the follow-up implementation of recommended programs. Hence, job satisfaction does not derive from the sense of being an organizational team player. The professional consultant's rewards vastly differ from those of the in-house executive. They include:

1

control over each assignment
diversity of tasks
control over one's time
freedom to be creative
freedom to disagree and criticize
freedom to live and work where one chooses

This list deserves closer examination, point by point.

Control over Each Assignment

The corporate employee has little, if any, control over assignments and tasks mandated by management, even if the employee disagrees with the need or merits of such an assignment. Tasks shuffle down the hierarchy in response to organizational needs and must be tackled promptly and accordingly. Rare is the security executive who has not grit teeth in frustration over dead-end, unproductive, or unnecessary assignments.

The consultant, as an independent professional, obviously is not so obliged. He or she may or may not accept an assignment, and the rejection of a specific task need not jeopardize the relationship with that client. If a consultant, for example, personally objects to spending time conducting statistical evaluations, she or he is free to reject such work and recommend someone else with appropriate skills to do it, and do it more efficiently, and at a lesser cost. Alternatively the task can be subcontracted to someone else.

That kind of control over one's work is, in and of itself, rewarding.

Diversity of Tasks

The security executive of a given firm devotes years focusing on one organization—or a given number of specific organizations, if the employer is a corporate or holding company. Put another way, the executive's view is limited and such limitations tend to narrow their perspective. There is only so much tinkering, so much organizational realignment, so much security manual updating, that can occur. And a company's security mission rarely if ever dramatically changes.

The security consultant's work is virtually limitless, even if the area of specialization is very narrow. Suppose a consultant specializes in retail security *exclusively*. The diversity in retail operations is staggering. Criteria would include

- type of merchandise being sold
- number of stores
- size of stores

- location of stores
- number of company employees
- size and organizational design of security department
- mission of security department (apprehension or prevention)
- warehouse and distribution system
- inventory shrinkage performance history
- known history of litigation problems

My own consulting practice is not restricted to retail, but in just that one specialty I have consulted a range of clients:

- a membership department store with seven stores, all located within 150 miles of each other
- an international mass-merchandiser
- a university's student store operation
- an exclusive Beverly Hills' retailer with only one store
- a drugstore chain in northern Mexico
- a fashion department store's regional division
- a Midwest discount chain with stores in several states
- a national shoe store firm
- a military post exchange
- a hardware store chain

Each of those retail consulting assignments had a different mission. Here are a few examples:

- One client had no formal or structured security department, so my task was to design one from the ground up, write a security manual, and outline job descriptions.
- One client wanted a structured training program for agents who specialized in detection and apprehension of shoplifters.
- One retailer wanted an audiovisual program for all employees to convey the message that security is everyone's responsibility.
- Another retailer limited the scope of my work to analyzing their distribution system for what they suspected was a faulty system that facilitated internal theft.
- Several retailers wanted to reduce inventory shrinkage without major organizational changes.

So, the diversity represented in the needs of each consultant's client makes for new challenges on an ongoing basis. Nothing becomes routine. No chance for burnout to occur. The horizons are limitless. The adventure of each day is the daily motivator. And the day's adventure proves to be the day's reward, the professional reward.

Control over One's Time

Rare is the person who does not count the days until vacation time or the holiday weekend. Such counting does not indicate dissatisfaction with one's career, but rather points up our longing for personal time, time not dictated by the company enterprise. The independent consultant truly owns and controls her or his own time. One of my colleagues simply refuses to schedule work one week each month; that week allows personal time for him and his family.

I do not so strictly regiment my time other than achieving a monthly goal of working 80 billable hours; but when a job involves travel I do set aside extra days to visit friends and relatives, to enjoy warm beaches or golf courses, to replenish my own wellspring of life.

Freedom to be Creative

Certainly, creative freedom varies from organization to organization. To suggest that security executives never enjoy such freedom would be erroneous. Yet, one cannot deny that more constraints exist within a given corporate culture, and employees can be inhibited about applying new ideas in solving old problems. Typically, the outside professional consultant is not influenced by those corporate constraints.

Management generally will consider recommendations and ideas from a consultant that would be rejected off-hand if suggested by members of the company's own staff. This is a phenomenon I do not fully understand, but it does happen.

Let us say that a consultant perceives that a company's line supervisors do not understand the role of security and do not support the protection program. Everyone, including the firm's security director, knows that supervisory support tends to bring about line employee acceptance of company programs. The objective, then, is to get the supervisors' support. Whereas the security director would not dare suggest that supervisors from various departments be included as observers in actual security investigations (to better understand the consequence of good security), the consultant could suggest such a radical idea. And that creative approach could meet with acceptance and implementation.

If senior management did not seek new, creative, dynamic suggestions and alternative ideas, they would not call in a consultant. If they had the solution to their problems in hand, they would not need a consultant.

The corporate security executive, no matter how talented he or she may be, must run out of new ideas in time. And many executives have learned that the conservative approach bears fewer risks in exposing oneself to ridicule or rejection. The consultant is new to the problem or challenge, and that freshness inspires new solutions. Furthermore, the consultant need not fear exposure or rejection, because a certain percentage of a consultant's work is usually rejected (recommendations not accepted or followed) in virtually every assignment.

This creativity is not limited to recommendations to clients. How the consultant manages her or his practice allows for the expression of a distinct personality and sense of creativity. That includes how books and records are maintained, how the work product (the consultant's final report) is packaged, and how projects are proposed. All facets of professional approach can reflect the individual businessperson. Security consulting is a new enough field that there are no wheel ruts in the road left by those who preceded us. There are, in fact, few roads.

Freedom to Disagree and Criticize

As oversimplified and perhaps trite as it may sound, executives are expected to agree and accept, while independent consultants are expected to disagree and criticize.

The corporate executive who criticizes management and the consultant who fully accepts a client's program will soon be headed for new career opportunities elsewhere.

This is not to suggest that consultants should seek confrontations or approach their clients as adversaries. Rather, they are obliged by virtue of their objectivity, independence, and professionalism to respond directly and honestly to a client's challenges. Straight talk is the consultant's privilege, right, freedom. It is a unique and rewarding experience to warn a client that he or she may not be happy with your assessment of their operation, while the client still encourages you to be candid.

I have been advised, in previous assignments, to avoid confronting the chief executive officer with what was perceived as the company's taboo topic, out of fear that my entire consulting project would be thrown out the corporate door. I have never been dissuaded from following my conscience and reporting my findings and, as sensitive as some issues have been, I have never suffered as a result of that honest commitment.

One retail firm, committed to reducing inventory shortages, retained me for guidance in that objective. One of their companywide problems was a lack of compliance with procedural controls. Company managers talked loud and long about the need for every employee to follow shortage prevention procedures, particularly to avoid paperwork errors. My survey disclosed that the company chairman was the worst offender of all. He would visit a store, make on-the-spot markdown decisions, and instruct store management to bypass the price-change procedure that would ensure a balance between book accounts and physical inventory. My report cited this problem and stated that if every employee was expected to follow the rules, the chairperson would have to set the example. No one else had been willing to confront the head of their company. Because of an outsider's report, however, he did refrain from some of those impulsive price changes and helped build a new atmosphere of shortage awareness at all levels in the company. The company's shortages have been on the decline ever since.

Another consulting project allowed me to work closely with a member of middle management who daily took exception to some of my critical observations and informal suggestions. That stalwart executive kept falling back on such statements as, "We've never done that before and our philosophy is to trust our employees," in response to my concern over insufficient preemployment screening. That executive, in fact, warned me that if some of my informal comments found their way into my formal written report, any future consulting assignments for me could be jeopardized. I had the freedom (and, I believe, the obligation) to indeed include those critical observations and appropriate remedies. I have not been retained for any more work for that company, but I would do it all over again![1] Every professional consultant that I can think of would do the same, too. Good news or bad news, that is what a consultant is all about.

Freedom to Live and Work Where One Chooses

One high mark earned by the consulting profession is the freedom to live and work anywhere one chooses. A security executive must live and work near the employer's facilities. Location can be the overriding factor in employment choices. If one wishes to rise to the level of a vice presidency and the opportunity presents itself in New Jersey, the qualified candidate must be willing to live there and forego the warm beaches of Florida. Independent security consultants are located in various cities throughout the United States because, for whatever reason, they choose to be there.

Just imagine, if you've always wanted to live on a golf course in the lovely mountains of northern San Diego, you may do so—and build a business, too.

THE CONSULTANT'S DAILY WORK

What is a consultant? The American Heritage Dictionary defines a *consultant* simply as (1) a person who gives expert or professional advice; (2) a person who consults another. The International Association of Professional Security Consultants (IAPSC) defines a consultant as a person who provides security advice, information, and recommendations to management.

To discover in more detail what distinguishes a *security consultant*, while once speaking to attendees at the IAPSC's annual meeting, I asked seminar participants (who represented both practicing consultants and prospective consultants) to jot down what they do. Their answers offer some meaningful insight to

---

[1] Three years subsequent to the publication of the first edition of this book and five years after that threat I was retained again by that corporation. The security executive, for reasons totally unconnected with me or my original report, had been down-graded in rank. The quality of my work prevailed in the long haul!

the work:

I gather information relating to the client's security arrangements, analyze vulner-abilities, prepare a report outlining our findings, and list recommendations to improve vulnerabilities.

I provide the benefit of my expertise to clients to assist them in identifying and controlling losses and reducing risks, as well as provide expert testimony.

Help corporate clients prevent crime and protect their assets ... and determine if security is adequate.

I see my function as a problem-solver, even to the extent of discovering a problem before the client knows one exists.

Assess risks and recommend cost-conscious programs to prevent loss of life and property.

Evaluate client's existing security situation and make recommendations for improving the situation within a reasonable time frame at an acceptable expense.

I develop solutions to security puzzles.

I shared with the attendees of that same conference the story of my very first appearance before a prospective client: I was ushered into a boardroom. Seated around a large and very beautiful, glossy table were half a dozen senior executives, rocking to and fro in large black leather chairs with high backs. A round of introductions followed, and then I was seated. I had been called there by one of the company's officers. I had not submitted any proposal, nor did I fully understand their security needs.

The chairperson, a delightful gentleman, wasted no time and succinctly put to me one question. I shall never forget his words, "Well now, Chuck, what are you going to do for us?" So, I posed the same question that that chairperson put to me and asked the attendees to quickly jot down what they would say. Following are a few of those responses:

I will give you the benefit of my experience in protecting your personnel and assets at a cost which will speak favorably to your profits.

I am going to analyze current security management practices in relationship to industry norms as I know them. I will then be in a position to verify those practices or recommend changes in your program.

Work with you to define the scope of your security problem. Propose an approach for getting information to evaluate that problem or problems, and present to you a series of alternatives to address those problems.

I will provide my expertise and experience to identify the existing factors of risk in your operation, analyze the risks, and provide my recommendations as to the measures to be taken to reduce, control, or transfer the risks.

I will provide an objective assessment of the company's/institution's security arrange-ments with recommendations for any needed improvements.

I'm going to guide you through the process of solving your problem by helping you organize available information, gather needed information, and utilize my experience in the process.

So, beyond the dictionary's definition, security consulting is in every sense of the word a *process*, a problem-solving process in which the consultant must first identify the problem(s), gather available data pertaining to the problem(s), analyze that data, and then offer advice in recommendations that will solve, cure, or otherwise minimize the problem(s). Sometimes consulting assignments do not require us to solve problems. Designing a security plan for a new enterprise, for example, a consultant will follow a problem-prevention process to guide the company into a secure future.

Other Examples of Consultant's Work/Tasks

Some years back while preparing for a national presentation on the topic of security consulting and what consultants do I prepared what I called my Alphabetical Soup of Consulting.

Perhaps you'll agree it does offer a rather interesting insight into those kinds of things we do in this profession.

A. Advise management on what's current, i.e., state of the art.
B. Build bridges between security and other departments.
C. Clarify and rewrite security policies, procedures, etc.
D. Define organizational goals and mission statements.
E. Expedite security projects.
F. Forecast protection needs in the future.
G. Guide management in its selection of equipment and services.
H. Help hire qualified security personnel.
I. Identify problems.
J. Judge past and present performance.
K. Kindle new enthusiasm or interest.
L. Launch new programs by conducting orientation meetings.
M Modify security operations when and where appropriate.
N. Negotiate, on behalf of management, for optimum contracts.
O. Objectively evaluate security programs, present and future.
P. Present new ideas and strategies.
Q. Qualify senior security candidates for management's consideration.
R. Review security budgets.
S. Supplement the security management staff on a temporary basis.
T. Train security employees.
U. Uncover unproductive policies, practices or programs.
V. Validate existing or planned activities.
W. Warn management of risks and unnecessary exposure.
Y. Yield unbiased and honest opinions.
Z. Zealously provide the highest order of professional assistance and guidance possible to each client.

These pursuits constitute a worthy profession indeed.

Chapter 2

Qualifications of a Professional Management Consultant

An attorney, accountant, teacher, or registered nurse has a clearly defined path of preparation to follow to earn that certain title. That is true with virtually any occupation. If a person deviated from the prescribed preparatory steps and yet claimed to be, say, an engineer, such person could be viewed as a fraud.

So, we live in a society where credentials are mandated. The credentials speak for the holder. No one, likely, would argue with the need to ensure that one is qualified to perform as promised.

However, there is no clearly defined path that qualifies one to be a consultant. There are no college or university programs that lead to a consulting undergraduate or graduate degree. There are no governmental regulatory bodies, like a state's board of medical examiners, to license consulting practitioners.

As a consequence, to become a consultant, all one must do is say, "I am." And some people do just that.

Irrespective of the absence of predetermined training, qualifications do exist. The one who truly is not qualified to perform as a consultant will soon be exposed and rejected.

There are four broad areas of competence that a consultant must achieve in order to be considered qualified. These four areas are:

- **experience**
- **education**
- **professional credentials**
- **personal and interpersonal skills**

EXPERIENCE

The ideal security consultant would possess some work experience in three consecutive tracks: *line* or functional experience, *supervisory* experience, and *managerial* experience. Let us look at each of these levels, one at a time.

Line Experience

The consultant should have worked, hands-on, in whatever specialty he or she claims expertise; for instance, I work in retail security and in that field of specialty, and I have personally lain up in ceiling plenum chambers for hours surveilling cash registers with a history of shortages and have observed dishonest employees manipulate sale and refund transactions. Following the observed thefts, I would personally interrogate the thief. That kind of line or functional experience is invaluable in consulting with a retail firm about the needs for detecting register theft.

Supervisory Experience

The supervisor is a genuine catalyst in the workforce, serving as a liaison between the line employee and management. He or she translates programs into action and, in reverse, points out problems of execution to the program designers. A consultant who has no experience in the "buffer zone" is at some disadvantage.

Another benefit of supervisory work is that one experiences personnel performance appraisal. Supervisors rate and measure performance of employees; that type of background contributes to later, overall understanding of a client's employee productivity needs.

Managerial Experience

This kind of experience is most valuable. How can one talk to managers, understand managers, identify with managers' concerns and problems, unless one has been there? How can the consultant appreciate budgetary constraints and budget battles unless he or she has smelled the gunpowder of the fight?

EDUCATION

Surely two years of college is the minimum amount of education required of a consultant. Those two years would have to include some emphasis on communication skills, writing skills, business law, accounting, and psychology. More ideally, the consultant should have a bachelor's degree in our profession, that is, security administration, security management, administration of justice, police science and administration, criminal justice, or whatever the institution of higher learning chooses to title the degree. Needless to say, advanced (graduate) degrees enhance one's credentials.

The value of one's education lies in what it represents in terms of work, commitment, and self-discipline. That speaks well for the woman or man who is advising others on how they should conduct their affairs. Also, the majority of people in managerial or executive positions in the companies for which you will work have earned degrees; right or wrong, they expect an outside consulting expert to be similarly educated.

PROFESSIONAL CREDENTIALS

Another dimension of professional activity exists beyond work and formal education; this I categorize as *professional credentials*. It includes such areas as public speaking, writing and publishing articles, membership in professional organizations, and professional certifications.

Public Speaking

A would-be consultant should seek out opportunities to speak publicly about security-related issues and topics. Such presentations are relatively easy to arrange with a wide variety of service organizations and professional groups that constantly seek fresh speakers with interesting topics. During the first year of my own consultancy, I relied on speaking honorariums as a source of income. However, whether or not a fee is paid remains unimportant in terms of building this base of qualifying experience that is so valuable in the consultant's background. Volunteering to speak or sit on a seminar panel presentation within our own industry—be it local chapter programs or national seminars and meetings—is another avenue to this speaking experience.

Writing and Publishing Articles

It may be fair to say that if you cannot write you cannot consult. Rare is the consulting project that does not result in a written final report of recommendations. I do not think I know one security consultant who has not published work in some magazine or newsletter.

The security industry has a variety of magazines and trade publications that are most willing to publish timely and well written articles by members of our profession and even outsiders. Such periodicals include *Security Management, Security, Security Technology & Design, Access Control, Journal of Security Administration, The Protection of Assets Manual, Protection Officer News*, to name a few in this country. Canada's *Security* and Great Britain's *International Security Review* also offer publishing opportunities.

Although there is clear and unmistakable value in having an article published in our industry, there's even more potential benefit, more bang for the buck so to speak, in writing for journals *outside* our profession. Why? Security publishers usually don't pay an honorarium for articles, other industries do. It would be unusual to get a consulting assignment as a result of an article in security publications, whereas you stand a good chance of being contacted for possible work as a consequence of your article in another profession's magazine. For example: I authored a relatively short article for *Cleaning and Restoration* (the official publication of the Association of Specialists in Cleaning & Restoration) entitled *Hiring the best, avoiding the rest* with the subtitle *Honest, hard-working employees will make you money. Dishonest ones will take your money. Here's how to hire the honest ones.* From that work I was compensated for writing it and it brought me consulting assignments.

To be able to provide a prospective client with a bibliography of articles you've published goes a long way in establishing your reputation as a professional.

If you are not published as you read this, set yourself a goal right now to write an article and get it published!

A would-be consultant must have a demonstrated track record of effectively communicating by way of the written word before he or she hangs out that consultant's shingle.

Membership in Professional Organizations

Membership in various professional organizations is not a measurement of one's gregarious nature but, rather, demonstrates an interest in what others are thinking and doing, the willingness to share with others, the involvement with activities that invariably spin off volunteer organizations, and an effort to stay current in one's own field of endeavor.

Good judgment dictates how many organizations to which one can reasonably and profitably belong. At this point in my career I only maintain membership in the International Association of Professional Security Consultants (IAPSC), the American Society for Industrial Security (ASIS), and the International Foundation for Protection Officers (IFPO). The first of these is extremely important to me because it serves my needs as a practicing consultant (it's a consultant's organization just for consultants), and the others are important because they service the industry in the broadest sense. That limited membership is by personal choice; many other fine security organizations exist. As time passes, more sharply defined organizations are emerging, with more focus on their own special problems, for example, the International Association for Hospital Security.

The point is, the consultant cannot exist in a vacuum. She or he can only benefit, even if in small measure, by affiliating with and sharing with peers, colleagues, and practitioners within the industry.

Professional Certifications

The vast majority of security consultants possess the protection industry's most coveted professional certification which is the Certified Protection Professional

(CPP) designation that follows one's name. This certification process is administered by ASIS. Although the testing and awarding of the certification is under the auspices of ASIS, membership in that society is not required. The test spans eight industry disciplines and requires a full day of testing by written examination to complete. A fee is charged.

Another industry-wide certification is the Certified Protection Officer (CPO) designation, as administered by the International Foundation for Protection Officers. This certification is earned through a correspondence program. A fee is charged.

Without question the most prestigious certification that can be obtained in the consulting profession, in my view, is the Certified Management Consultant (CMC) obtainable under the auspices of the Institute of Management Consultants located in New York City. A candidate for the CMC designation must take a written examination, appear before an oral board of consulting peers and submit a list of prior clients who are queried as to the quality and effectiveness of her/his work. This is the professional hallmark for consultants in all disciplines, not just security consultants. As of this writing only four security consultants are so certified, including this author.

PERSONAL AND INTERPERSONAL SKILLS

As fundamental as it is and as obvious as it may appear, there are some important factors about each of us, as human beings and as individuals, that enhance or impede the business of consulting. Those skills or qualities include:

- integrity and honesty
- demeanor
- patience
- persuasive powers
- grooming
- self-confidence

Integrity and Honesty

The man or woman who seeks a career in consulting, particularly in the security industry, must be an impeccably honest person of deep integrity. The opportunities for a wide range of unethical and dishonest practices far exceed those in most professions. It is easy to cheat on billing clients because verification is almost if not indeed impossible. Clients must have confidence that proprietary information is not shared with competitors or any outsiders. Regrettably, some consultants have failed in this area, just as other professionals have fallen in theirs.

Demeanor

The consultant is invited into the true inner sanctums of business and industry, where social graces and expectations are at the highest levels. Just hours after sitting in the finest of leather chairs on only the finest of Persian carpets, sipping coffee from bone china, I have been probing trash dumpsters with janitors and line security officers. If you conduct yourself with confidence and with due respect to all concerned, you will find yourself accepted equally by the cast of characters at both ends of the organizational spectrum.

Patience

There is a time to hustle and a time to wait, and the consultant who understands timing is a person of patience. Organizational delays are the most frustrating of all, primarily because your "meter is running" and valuable time is being wasted—not by your choice but by the organization's.

Hence, patience is required in awaiting decisions, meetings and appointments, information and materials you need to progress in your analysis, and action promised as well as action required for the analysis. Example: one client was wasting money by hiring off-duty police officers part-time to guard cash office operations in each store. My recommendation was to reduce those payroll expenses and physically modify the cashier offices. A couple of years elapsed before management decided to incur the one-time capital expenditure to remodel the offices and do away with the exorbitant payroll costs.

Persuasive Powers

It only stands to reason that the consultant is going to suggest change. If change was not deemed a remote possibility, then a consultant would not have been called to the scene. So, change more often that not is an inevitable consequence of the consulting process. Yet, human nature being what it is, people resist change. Many decisions in an organization are the responsibility of a collective group such as the executive committee. Some members may favor the change while others oppose it. The gentle art of persuasion on the part of the consultant tends to expedite change.

Grooming

We are all guilty of the tendency to judge others based on their appearance. How we present ourselves in dress and personal grooming can make the difference between gaining or losing the contract. Conservative business suits and ties, polished shoes, good taste in accessories, all say something about the person. A casual shirt or flashy tie belongs at the race track, not the boardroom.

Self-confidence

I don't know how a person could survive as a consultant if they lacked self-confidence. Those who seek out an expert (and that is what a consultant really is, an expert in a given area) expect the expert to be in full command of the topical area in question and move to resolve the issue with confidence. Confidence is a quality that is exuded, that is discernible to those around us. If you don't know your stuff, if you don't feel good about yourself and what you can do, it'll show. The lesson here: don't take on tasks you are not qualified to handle—that's one form of self-confidence!

Finally, all the foregoing is offered with the belief the would-be consultant has a skill to offer, an expertise to share. That goes without saying. The independent and professional security consultant has absolutely nothing to sell or offer other than his or her experience, advice, and good judgment. Those "commodities," if I may use that word, are the very underpinning, the foundation, upon which the consulting practice is built. This chapter has addressed the other qualifications.

Chapter 3

Ten Most Common Questions Asked about Entering the Profession

The questions people ask concerning career opportunities in security consulting tend to become repetitive. I have condensed those questions into the ten most commonly or frequently asked, and here I offer some answers:

Question #1: OF ALL THE THINGS ONE SHOULD DO TO BE SUCCESSFUL, WHICH WOULD BE THE MOST IMPORTANT TO ACHIEVE SUCCESS?

Answer: There's more than one quality, characteristic or value necessary for success. Perhaps the most important would be integrity, closely followed by impeccable quality of work. Then would come the need for calm self-confidence, even in the face of worrisome problems and obstacles, all bound together with a real dedication to succeed. And lastly but certainly not least, one must have the self-discipline to attack the work and get it done.

Question #2: HOW MUCH TIME AND MONEY ARE REQUIRED TO OPEN A CONSULTANCY?

Answer: That is a good question, because time is equated with money. My understanding when I started my own business was that I should be prepared to support myself financially for one year. That arbitrary figure is misleading, however. I think my colleagues would agree it takes longer than twelve months to become financially established and secure.

Unless the consultant begins with a handful of corporate retainers to guarantee income, or unless you open the doors for business with a major contract in hand, it would be prudent to plan on *building* your reputation and practice for the first one and a half to two years.

Financial requirements for a new business are very subjective. Money, for the independent as well as the corporate budget, is divided into three categories:

1. payroll (your salary)
2. sundry expenses (stationery supplies, printing, telephone expenses, travel, etc.)
3. capital expenditures (desk, personal computer, file cabinets, etc.)

Operating out of one's home, which I do, reduces costs considerably. So, I started with odds-and-ends and one typewriter, and I was off and running with an initial investment, including my printing costs, of less than $2,000. Today, with a personal computer, probably $6,000–$7,000 would be more realistic. Then you must stay afloat until the cash flow exceeds your former income level. Your most immediate goal is to generate an income that matches the salary of your last job.

How do you stay afloat? You should be prepared to bankroll or support yourself for about eighteen months. If you were earning $65,000 as a security director or as a deputy chief of police, you should have at least that amount, and probably half again that much, on which to draw. You will hope not to use it up, but it must be available in one form or another as a cash reserve. Certainly one advantage of that reserve has to do with a sense of financial security, an important psychological factor, particularly in view of the probable fact that you have *always* had a salary to count on and now you do not.

Question #3: HOW DOES SOMEONE KNOW IF HE OR SHE CAN MAKE A LIVING BY BEING A SECURITY CONSULTANT?

Answer: Others do it, so why can't you? The only way to really know is to try it. Surely indicators have surfaced during your career that would suggest the likelihood of your success. Have you solved problems that brought you recognition? Have you developed a plan or program that earned you a reputation as an innovator or achiever? Have others seen you as a leader, a risk-taker, or a creative manager?

The successful consultant of today probably demonstrated such qualities while serving as a practitioner.

Question #4: HOW DOES SOMEONE GO ABOUT MARKETING THEIR CONSULTING SKILLS?

Answer: Chapter 5 is devoted to this topic.

Question #5: IS PRIOR LAW ENFORCEMENT EXPERIENCE VALUABLE?

Answer: Law enforcement is but one of six major professions for dealing with crime in society. Those six are:

1. the criminologist, who studies the causation of crime
2. the security specialist, who attempts to prevent crime from occurring

3. the police specialist, who enforces criminal law, including the detection and apprehension of the person who commits the crime
4. the judiciary, who deals with the innocence and guilt of suspected criminal offenders
5. the correctional specialist, who deals with the incarceration of the criminal
6. probation and parole people, who deal with offenders on a post-release basis

Although they share one common target, crime, they each have totally different missions. One who excels in one of these fields will not be guaranteed the same level of success in another.

But I do feel prior experience in law enforcement can be valuable if not essential. I commenced my career in police service and it has benefited me.

Question #6:   WOULD IT BE A GOOD IDEA TO FIND WORK IN ANOTHER MANAGE-MENT CONSULTING ORGANIZATION BEFORE TRYING TO BREAK INTO SECURITY CONSULTING?

Answer: Certainly any consulting experience would help, but it seems to me such strategy defeats the very purpose of considering entering into an independent consultancy. One of the major attractions to being a consultant is the independence and freedom it affords.

Question #7:   WHERE WOULD ONE FIND SECURITY CONSULTING STANDARDS TO ENSURE ONE IS OPERATING IN THE MAINSTREAM?

Answer: There are no published *consulting standards* as such. There is a growing body of "custom and practice" guidelines, best accessed through the International Association of Professional Security Consultants (IAPSC). Membership, attendance at the annual meeting, and personal contacts and friendships plug one into what is happening in the business. That association has published a Code of Ethics which can serve, in some measure, as a guideline (see Chapter 11).

There simply is no substitute for personal contacts and the exchange of ideas. As an independent consultant, I found myself alone and in need of colleagues and their thoughts. To this day, I seek out the advice or good counsel of other consultants, even if only to reaffirm something I am doing or thinking of doing.

The Institute of Management Consultants, Inc., also has published a Code of Professional Conduct and offers a certification program for management consultants.

Question #8:   IS THERE ANY FORMULA BY WHICH A FLEDGLING CONSULTANT CAN MEASURE THE VALUE OF HER OR HIS WORTH?

Answer:　　　　The late Howard L. Shenson, known as the consultants' consultant, has provided the best formula, in my judgment. In essence, your fee should be based on:

1.　Direct labor (the value of your service)
2.　Overhead (about 45% of your labor cost)
3.　Profit (about 15% of your labor and overhead)

Let us look more closely on each of these three components of the fee:

Direct Labor (the value of your service)

- You just left a position that paid $65,000.
- You worked 241 days (3 weeks' vacation, 6 holidays, and weekends off).
- Divide your salary of $65,000 by 241 working days and the value of each day worked was $270 per day.
- Add benefits of at least 30% to the daily worth, or $81, because benefits are part of the compensation package although not reflected in the salary figure.

Hence: $270 + $81 = $351 per day. That was your daily worth when working 241 days a year. BUT YOU ARE *NOT* GOING TO WORK EVERY DAY AS A CONSULTANT!

- Estimate the number of days you will work *FOR A FEE* in the coming year. Use 140 days as an example.
- Divide your former salary of $65,000 by 140 days, which amounts to $464 plus the 30% benefit amount.

Hence: $464 + $139 = $603 per day. So as to maintain the same income and only work 140 days, your daily value is $603.

　　　　But it costs you money to conduct your own business so you must charge those costs, known as overhead, to your daily worth or value.

Overhead

A sampling of overhead costs looks like this:

	monthly	annually
Clerical assistant	$200	$2,400
Phone	300	3,600
Travel	400	4,800
Insurance	160	1,920
Postage/shipping/supplies	100	1,200
Marketing	600	7,200
Entertainment	100	1,200
Dues & subscriptions	100	1,200
Legal & accounting	125	1,500
Miscellaneous	100	1,200
	$2,185	$26,220

- Divide the annual overhead costs by the number of days you expect to work, i.e., $26,220 divided by 140 days equals $187.

DIRECT LABOR (value of your daily service)	$603.00
OVERHEAD	187.00
	790.00
PROFIT (@ 15%)	118.00
	908.00

- Your daily fee as a fledgling consultant = $908.00

Now, these numbers are hypothetical and do not necessarily reflect a given consultant's operating circumstances. And note the absence of office rent or janitorial service, two expenses that must be considered if the office is not in your home. But the formula does give a rough guideline in response to the question.

I have talked to many new consultants and typically they are charging too low a fee, a fee that sooner or later will force them out of business.

For your information, security consultants' fees currently range between $750 and $2,000 per day, with most professionals charging between $1,000 and $1,600.

Question #9: DO YOU HAVE TO MAINTAIN A PARALLEL CAREER IN ACADEMIA OR BUSINESS IN ORDER TO KEEP ABREAST OF INDUSTRY ADVANCES?

Answer: I lectured on a part-time basis for thirteen years at California State University at Los Angeles, but when I embarked upon a consulting career I could not continue at the university because of the uncertainties of my weekly availability. It was not possible to make a commitment to teach every Wednesday evening when I was, at the same time, advertising myself as prepared to work anywhere in the world for any client at any time.

Teaching or working part-time in some security-related business is not how one keeps abreast of industry advances. That is accomplished by reading the trade journals; participating in appropriate associations; communicating with practitioners, colleagues, and peers; and reading the books published for our security industry.

Question #10: IS THERE AN AVERAGE PERIOD OF TIME OVER WHICH ONE MUST PRACTICE BEFORE REALIZING PROFESSIONAL RECOGNITION AND FINANCIAL SUCCESS?

Answer: That's a tough one! I am sure some of my established colleagues have various opinions on the definition of recognition and success. My best answer is that the first one to three years are the leanest. They represent the building years, the time one struggles not only for client acceptance but for recognition within the industry. My experience and the experience of some of my closest friends in this business indicates that the curve is on an ever-upward incline. This year represents my sixteenth anniversary as an independent security consultant, and my business has grown every year but two since I opened my doors.

Recognition comes when someone you met at an IAPSC meeting or through other professional networks phones you for advice or refers a prospective client to you. Financial success is perhaps the most difficult to adequately define. This is subjectively interpreted. I can say that I know security consultants whose income exceeds the highest-paid security executives in the country. That being the case, at what point between commencing the consultancy and this maximum financial achievement can one say they are successful? Everyone must determine their own standards.

Chapter 4

Starting the Business

Once one has decided to become an independent consultant, the second decision is whether to incorporate or operate as a sole proprietor.

I and the majority of consultants I know chose the sole practitioner route, principally because it is the least cumbersome, easier, and less expensive. I consulted with an attorney friend at the outset about incorporating and he assured me there was no particular advantage to do so. Each year thereafter I again would broach the subject and his position remained the same: Why bother? You don't need to and you don't want to! I listened to his advice. In your future you'll hope your clients listen to yours! In any event, if you have questions about which way to go, consult with an attorney.

Hence, I encourage this entrepreneurial venture be approached as a sole practitioner with no staff, at least at the outset. As your business grows you may wish to add a secretary or research assistant or even another consultant, if you choose. On the other hand I have now been a consultant for 16 years, am recognized as being quite successful and remain unincorporated with no employees. After all, I left an excellent management position to be free and independent; to add staff would only put me back into a management position again.

With that aside, let's now consider a host of other decisions and actions that, when completed, will allow you to open your doors for business. They include:

geographic location of the business
specific location of office
telephone service
naming the business
press release
bank account
business record keeping
office equipment
stationery

We will examine these areas, one at a time.

GEOGRAPHIC LOCATION OF THE BUSINESS

Most of us consultants started our business in the cities in which we live; probably for two reasons. First, we assumed that a significant percentage of our business would come from within that community. Second, the trauma of this radical career change along with the trauma of relocating to a strange community would be too much to ask of oneself, let alone one's family.

It would not *hurt* to consider relocating to a city that could serve more effectively as a hub of operations for your work. If your specialty happens to be in the security of petroleum refineries, oil drilling site security, and the transportation of petroleum or crude, it would not make a lot of sense to open an office in New York.

However, my office is in San Diego County, California, and I have relatively few clients in San Diego. As a matter of fact, I seriously considered moving to Omaha, Nebraska early in my consulting career because it simply made more sense to be there in the center of the country than in one corner, but my heart overrode my good sense and I stayed in Southern California. Surely some potential clients opted not to hire me due to travel costs, but I have survived those losses.

There is something to be said about being close to your market and something to be said about living and working from exactly where you want to live. Corporate employees cannot have that luxury!

SPECIFIC LOCATION OF OFFICE

If you can spare a room in your home and convert it into an office, that is a prudent way to begin. One obvious advantage is convenience. Plus, it reduces your operating costs (overhead). Also, the Internal Revenue Service permits the businessperson who has an office in the home to write off a portion of the home rental or mortgage payment as an office expense.

A caution is in order here: You must have a great deal of self-discipline to operate out of your home because of constant distractions and temptations to wander away from the office into another part of the house. The convenience of the office in the home is a two-edged sword. I always have operated from my home, and from the first day I have kept business hours of 9 A.M. to 5 P.M. *minimum*, *religiously*, Monday through Friday. More often than not, I am at my desk before 8 A.M.

For those who opt for a more formal office arrangement, two common strategies exist. First, you could rent office space in a building in which not only workspace but typical office amenities are included, such as a receptionist who, among other tasks, answers your phone in your absence. This receptionist serves a pod or grouping of offices. This sort of office typically has access to a small conference room in which you can meet with clients. Other amenities of this rental agreement would include copier and typing services, janitorial service, and office security. All in all, it is a neat package that certainly gives the consultant the appearance of success and professionalism.

The other option is the renting or leasing of the more traditional office, in which you hire your own secretary/receptionist who serves you exclusively. This is the most cumbersome option for the sole proprietor—and certainly is the most expensive.

TELEPHONE SERVICE

The telephone is perhaps the most vital tool of your business, because without a phone you are out of touch and unavailable to anyone who may be seeking your counsel. Indeed, the phone is more important than the office. You need a business telephone line (as opposed to a residential line). The phone company will list the name and number of your business in the classified yellow pages under *security consultants*, a relatively new subcategory under the major heading of *security*. Other possibilities include *security guard & patrol service*, *security control equipment*, and *systems and security systems consultants* (typically fire and burglar alarm companies). The regular alpha listing is free. Available at a charge are bold type alpha listings and display ads.

Some businesses would be hard-pressed to survive without a yellow pages' listing in the local directory. My experience tells me it is important to be listed, but most of my business comes from other marketing and advertising strategies, such as referrals.

Telephone Equipment

If the office is in your home, you will need a separate business line and at least one phone instrument. Depending on the size and layout of the house, you may wish to have a second business instrument to signal your business calls when you are in another area of the house. A cordless phone works well, too, to let you sit by the pool or on the front deck and still deal with calls coming in on the business line.

My own office has a speakerphone that lets me engage in phone conversations with my hands free.

Additionally, I have *call waiting* service, whereby while I am engaged in a phone conversation with one party, an audible signal tells me that another call is coming in. This efficient, low-cost service is worth its weight in gold because it allows you to conduct business with only one business line, yet to accept incoming calls as though you had multilines.

I also use *call forwarding* to send incoming calls into my *voice mail* when I'm not in the office or unable to answer my phone or am out of the office. Works like a charm!

FACSIMILE COVER SHEET
FROM

CHARLES A. SENNEWALD & ASSOCIATES

TO

NAME: _____

FIRM: _____

FAX # _____

SUBJECT _____

Page _____ of _____ pages.

MESSAGE (IF ANY) _____

_____

_____

_____

_____

_____

Date _____

CHARLES A. SENNEWALD & ASSOCIATES
SECURITY MANAGEMENT CONSULTING
28004 LAKE MEADOW DRIVE
ESCONDIDO, CALIFORNIA 92026

619 / 749-7527
FAX 619 / 749-3032

FIGURE 4–1   *Facsimile cover sheet.*

The telephone facsimile machine (FAX) is an indispensable piece of office equipment today. It allows for immediate transmission of written documents that can often make a critical difference in your business.

Answering the Phone

Unless you have a secretary or other employee dedicated to answering the telephone every business day throughout the year, you must subscribe to an answering service or utilize an answering machine. Both have their drawbacks.

The telephone answering machine answers your incoming calls with your prerecorded message. You can remotely access the messages if you are out of town. This system does work, and a number of my colleagues use such equipment. I personally had the frustration of a mechanical failure and lost some messages, so I changed over to an answering service.

Answering services provide their own peculiar frustrations for their subscribers, like transposing phone numbers, neglecting to give you your messages when you call in for them, and misunderstanding the sound of the caller's name. For example, the answering service informs you of a call from a Ms. Betcurns. You call Ms. Betcurns and the secretary advises no such person is at that number. You tell her you are returning a call taken by your answering service and they tend to misunderstand the phonetics of names. The secretary understands, and the two of you conclude that the call must have emanated from Ms. Betty Karens of their office. The answering service is, nonetheless, a bargain, and some are operated quite professionally.

I've used an answering machine as well as a professional answering service but today use my phone company's voice mail service. In a sense, it is a combination of the other two options with this advantage: the phone company's equipment is professional and will not fail, and I feel the consultant's own message, assuming he has a good speaking voice, actually has a positive influence on the caller.

NAMING THE BUSINESS

Three options are available in naming a new consulting business. The first is simply to use one's own name with a description of the business:

JOAN P. JONES
    Consultant—Criminology
    Police Procedures—Private Security

EDWARD B. SMITH
    Security Management and Litigation Consultant

The second option is to include one's name in the name of the business:

JOAN P. JONES & ASSOCIATES
SMITH AND ASSOCIATES, INC.

The last option is when the consultant names the business with a descriptive title that suggests the nature of his or her consultancy:

STRATEGIC AUDIT INC.
SECURITY CONCEPTS & SERVICES
APPLIED SECURITY SYSTEMS

State and local laws apply to establishing and conducting business. The authorities will provide direction and outline the nominal legal requirements.

PRESS RELEASE

The formation of a new business requires some form of announcement. You may purchase institutional advertisement space in trade journals, request free exposure in trade journals, send a formal printed announcement to prospective clients around the country, and garner some free publicity in your local newspaper.

A typical free announcement found in *Security Management* magazine's "Around the Industry" section under the *Security Observer* heading might read as follows:

> Ellen L. Smith, CPP, has formed a security management consultant practice called Security Management Guidance Services, Inc., and will serve as its president. The company will he located at 4000 Hilldrop Dr., Los Angeles, CA 90017. The phone number is 213/555–2020.

The objective, of course, is to let people know that you have changed identities and are now available as a consultant.

BANK ACCOUNT

Establish a checking account under the firm's name. Many banks will not extract a checking service charge if you maintain an agreed-upon minimum balance. And some banks will pay interest on your average balance. So you can write checks for free and earn interest at the same time. Only business-related expenses, including your own salary, should be written against this account.

BUSINESS RECORD KEEPING

I maintain two sets of records, a daily business journal and a financial journal.

Daily business journal: a 300-page, ten-by-twelve inch bound book, in which I make daily notations as to business activities. Sample entry for January 8:

> Made Retail Loss Prevention presentation to the winter International Consumer Electronic Show at the Las Vegas Convention Center for the agreed-upon flat fee.

This is not a required business activity but, I have found it useful for experiential and historical reference. I also use it to record my automobile mileage—a security measure against IRS audit.

Financial journal: all financial transactions, disbursements, and receipts are entered in a twenty-four-column journal, as depicted in Figure 4-2. This is the classical, old-fashioned way to keep financial records. More modern methods and software programs are available for one's personal computer. This detailed record is vital to one's business.

As indicated in Figure 4–2, every entry is made at least twice, that is, as a bank deposit or withdrawal *and* where that particular debit or credit belongs as a defined expense or type of income. Each column is totaled at the end of each month. Monthly totals can be recorded and compared for trends.

These records are indispensable in the preparation of your taxes and would be valuable documents in the event of an IRS audit (supported by the source's document, i.e., invoice or bill).

OFFICE EQUIPMENT

Following is a list of equipment recommended in starting a consulting business:

- personal computer and printer
- electronic typewriter (with memory, if possible) or word processor
- copier
- legal size 4-drawer filing cabinet
- video camera and VCR
- desk (with side bar to accommodate a computer or word processor) with chairs
- bookshelves to hold security industry library
- small audio recorder
- FAX machine
- cellular phone

FIGURE 4–2 Financial transactions, disbursement, and receipts recorded in a 24-column journal.

	DATE		CHECK NO.	BANK DEPOSITS	CHECKS	CASH DISBURSEMENTS	CONSULTING	HONORARIUM	ROYALTIES	OTHER INCOME	SECRETARY SERVICES	TELEPHONE	ADVERTISING
1	3-3-95	DEPOSIT (BLUE DOT DRUGS 1,500.00 / WHITE CO. 1,992.00)		349200			349200						
2	3-4-95	U.S. POSTMASTER	1531		4700								
3	3-7-95	AT&T	1532		30741							30741	
4	3-7-95	AMERICAN EXPRESS	1533		170582								
5	3-13-95	ESCONDIDO EXCHANGE	1534		15000						15000		
6	3-15-95	DEPOSIT (MILLER & MILLER 1000.00 / UCLA 1500.00)		250000			100000	150000					
7	3-17-95	THE GLOBE	1535		15000								15000
8	3-21-95	SHELL OIL				21178							
9	3-22-95	CONNIE SEHNEWALD	1536		200000								
10													
11													
12													
13													
14													
15													
16													
17													
18													

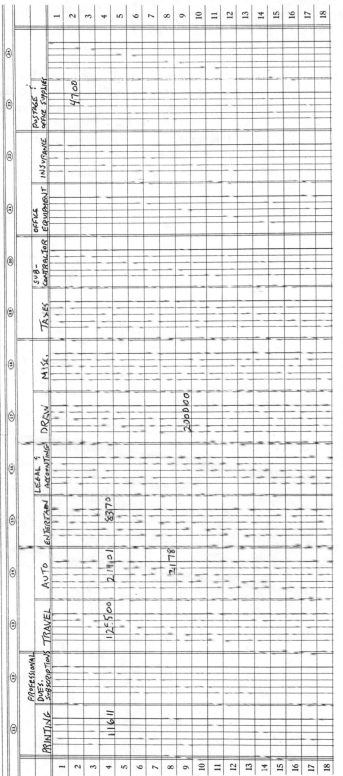

FIGURE 4-2 Continued.

STATIONERY

Once the name of your firm has been established, a graphic artist can develop an appropriate logo, should you desire one, for inclusion on your letterhead and advertising materials. Or if you choose not to have a logo, a graphic specialist can recommend a professional layout for your letterhead and business card.

Care must be taken in this seemingly simple task, because your stationery says something about you and your service. Tasteful layout of the letterhead, and quality paper and printing all suggest a top-notch business.

Chapter 5

Marketing

Given the various aspects of consulting, marketing may seem most foreign to those who begin security consulting. To market, after all, is to offer oneself for sale, and that is essentially what marketing is: to offer for sale. People in the security industry engaged in selling a product or service have historically been viewed as *vendors*, second class citizens in terms of membership status in professional societies and associations, not in the mainstream of the profession. Vendors offer products that may or may not work, services that may or may not perform as claimed, and now the new consultant is faced with this strange orientation of being the supplier of services as opposed to the purchaser of services. Still, the consultant is faced with the reality that marketing is a necessity.

Marketing, in the broadest sense, means deciding who your clients or best prospects are, and then deciding how to reach those prospective clients. That process requires three steps:

defining your services
identifying your customers
determining how you will reach those customers

DEFINING YOUR SERVICES

Defining your services is what gives you a unique identity. Following are actual statements of services offered by well-known, established consultants and each consultant's prospective customer base:

CONSULTANT #1: Survey of existing protection programs. Analysis of needs in development of corporate security, domestic and multinational. Vulnerability assessment of existing facilities: conceptual plans for new construction. Advisors in protection of trade secret information as well as for classified programs. Key personnel protection including risk recognition and scenario preparation for crisis management exercises. Guidance in litigation avoidance.

Prospective clients: architects and designers; manufacturing and distribution; financial, educational, and healthcare institutions;

utilities and military services energy sources; data processing centers.

CONSULTANT #2: Security/loss prevention audits and surveys. Implementation of loss-control programs. Security/loss prevention seminars for front-line supervisors, including awareness programs. Specialize in consulting for firms who do not employ full-time security professionals. Expert witness for security-related litigation.

Prospective clients: transportation; warehousing; distribution; industrial; hotel and restaurants.

CONSULTANT #3: Conducts a comprehensive study of an organization's security arrangements and equipment, including operations of the security department. Its objective is to identify vulnerabilities and recommend a level of security protective of people and property. Also provided are security seminars for bank employees.

Prospective clients: financial, healthcare, and educational institutions; businesses and industrial firms.

CONSULTANT #4: Specializes in safety, emergency management, and disaster recovery planning and training. Produces: special studies, audits, hazard analyses, risk assessments, emergency response and disaster recovery programs, crisis management guidelines and training for executives, emergency response procedures, and employee training. Industrial mutual aid management training and plan reviews by government agencies are also produced.

Prospective clients: corporations, governments, and nonprofit organizations.

CONSULTANT #5: Conducts in-depth security surveys; reviews existing security operation and defines needs to the unique infrastructure of the organization surveyed; develops recommendations to facilitate loss prevention. Cost reduction "value surveys." Specializes in design and specification of computer-based alarm/access control systems and security training and policy development. Considerable clientele of architects and other consultants. Extensive experience in museum, historic property, corporate art collections, and operations/training manuals. Firm includes fire protection and electrical engineers and other associates.

Prospective clients: corporate security; museums, libraries, archives, historic properties; colleges and universities; hotels, condominiums; special services to architects and engineers; extensive computer datafile of specifications/bid documents for all types of security equipment.

CONSULTANT #6: Conducts security surveys to identify organizational strengths and weaknesses in protection and loss-prevention programs and makes cost-effective recommendations to cure or reduce deficiencies and maximize committed resources. Has proven track record of reducing inventory shrinkage in both common stock inventory and individual store accountability in inventory operations.

Prospective clients: retailers, manufacturing facilities; office/high-rise buildings, parking facilities (surface, subterranean, multilevel ramps), and security organizations (departments) in any environment.

It should be apparent, then, that defining one's services should be limited to no more than a single paragraph. It should also be apparent that the security consultant tends to have a particular strength in one area of protection but has, by virtue of experience, other peripheral skills as well. Consultant #6, above, offers the following expertise:

1. Primary strength is in retail security.
2. By virtue of experience in retail, has developed skills in conducting surveys that identify needs.
3. Has skills in manufacturing, primarily due to inventory-control experience in retailing.
4. Probably developed skills in office and high-rise buildings based on broad retail background in which retail outlets, corporate offices, and distribution centers were in such facilities.
5. Has skills in parking areas, based on experience of retail stores being necessarily connected with parking facilities.
6. Has skills in security organization management, based on years of managing a large security department.

And finally, it should be apparent that most skills are generic, that is, most security consultants can do what others can do, and only within a rather narrow area of specialization does the individual consultant have identity. Hence, that identity must be clearly defined.

IDENTIFYING YOUR CUSTOMERS

The problem with independent consulting is the tendency to see the world as one's oyster—everyone is a prospective client. But how is that a problem? It is far better to be overly optimistic than start off with a defeatist attitude. The problem lies not in overoptimism but in a failure to focus or channel one's marketing efforts toward the most likely prospects.

Let us say the new consultant has skills in retail drugstore security. Future customers will be drugstores, from major chains to single store operators. Everything the consultant does, once that customer is identified, sells the consulting service to that specific market. As a natural consequence of servicing, initially, that small segment of the whole retail market, the consulting practice

could then broaden to include other retailers, such as:
- specialty stores
- grocery stores
- convenience stores
- mass merchandisers and other front-end retailers
- department stores

The consultant must decide how broad the scope of the marketing effort should be. Probably the natural sequence would be to focus on drugstores and expand from there as quickly as possible, so as not to be locked into a restricted niche. The overall strategy would be to grow the expertise in drugstore retail security to general retail security. How do you do that? Seek out or create visibility by participating in retail loss-prevention workshops for shopping center merchants associations, chambers of commerce, local college sponsored programs for merchants, state retail association annual seminars, and other locally sponsored programs that offer the consultant a speaker's honorarium (or do it *pro bono*, free). Such exposure invariably leads to one's professional growth and consulting assignments.

The world *is* your oyster if you establish yourself as a competent professional who indeed can bring to the client viable solutions to security problems. Hard work enables one to transcend the original focus or market. An accomplished retail security consultant, for example, could land a small assignment in a local hospital's gift shop. That job could lead to a hospital administrators' request to survey their food service and commissary operation. Then the contract grows to a full survey of the hospital's security department and facility loss-prevention effort. That hospital consulting assignment leads to another local hospital assignment. And so it goes.

DETERMINING HOW YOU WILL REACH THOSE CUSTOMERS

The trick is not so much in how to reach the decision makers in your industry, because professional guidance is available to every consultant in the form of marketing consultants and services. Rather, your most challenging task will be to decide what message to send to potential clients. The message is paramount. The message will open doors or it will not.

Why would a retail executive opt to hire a security consultant—particularly if the organization already has a security manager or director? It is no surprise that management will spend money for one principal reason: to increase profitability. Retailers can increase profits by reducing inventory shrinkage or reducing operating costs. Hence, your marketing message to the retail executive must positively motivate that person to act, because you will increase their profitability through a loss-prevention awareness strategy. Conversely, you could negatively motivate the decision maker to act, because the erosion of company profits will only worsen unless positive changes are made under the guidance and assistance of a professional consultant.

This strategy applies, regardless of the area of specialty. Newspapers recently carried the story of a major theft of priceless works of art from a European art gallery. That loss apparently was the result of the gallery director's decision to reduce the security staff. The consultant's marketing message in this situation would easily hit its target.

Similarly, hardly a month goes by without news of a security failure in or outside the defense industry. These stories can provide good material for the consultant's message to prospective clients.

The real bottom line of the marketing effort is to develop a message that assures potential clients of a benefit that will be realized when your services are retained. The benefit in retailing is increased profits. The benefit in museums or art galleries is the preservation of works of art. The benefit in defense research and development is the protection of classified and proprietary data.

Bear this in mind because I view it as an axiom of consulting: *Most security consulting assignments are incident driven.* That is to say, something has happened within the organization that motivates senior management to incur the expense of bringing in an outside expert to cause some change which would be viewed as beneficial. Organizational "happenings" could include a significant change in top executives, an accident, a major criminal incident, an internal scandal, a civil lawsuit, the mysterious disappearance of equipment, property or inventory, the loss of a key employee, and so on. Any of these kinds of incidents could make an organization a prospective client.

The magic question is: How does one reach these prospective clients? Some marketing strategies include the following:

advertising

brochures

public appearances

direct mailings

business cards

promotional sundries

authorship

newsletters

pro bono **work**

Advertising

Traditional advertising strategies in our industry include classified and display ads in (1) security journals and (2) trade publications within our targeted market. The primary advantage of ads in security journals is keeping your name and availability as a security consultant alive. Trade publications, such as *Stores* magazine, a journal for retail executives, expose your service and availability directly to that targeted industry. Display advertising, which is substantially more expensive than classified ads, must convey a clear message. Interestingly, it seems that few security consultants advertise today in security trade journals.

A common question asked by those starting up new businesses has to do with how much one should spend on advertising. According to Troy's *Almanac of Business and Industrial Financial Ratios*, 1% of total revenue should be spent on advertising costs.

Brochures

A high-quality company brochure, preferably in color, has unquestionable impact on many potential buyers of consulting services. Brochures must be prepared by professional public relations or advertising artists. They must include:

- qualifications of the principal consultant (and associates, if any)
- experience as a consultant and practitioner
- range of consulting services offered, e.g., surveys, training sessions, security manuals
- length the consulting service has been in existence
- industries served

There are definitely two schools of thought about listing previous clients. Some believe it inappropriate to advertise the fact their former clients required consulting services. Others disagree with this philosophy and wish to disclose former clients. Just remember that if you choose to list clients, you must have their written consent. Brochures can be very costly to produce and care must be taken in their distribution. Because each brochure has value to you, you might try to direct your postal efforts so that the brochure gets into the hands of the firm's decision maker only.

Public Appearances

Seek speaking or panel slots on programs within your targeted market. Initially, those appearances may not pay a stipend; however, the important thing is to gain the exposure. Have something to contribute other than the same old meat and potatoes so frequently offered at industry seminars. Be creative, be thoughtful, be provocative, be original, be a presenter who stimulates the attendees' imagination.

Seek the opportunity to appear on early-morning radio talk shows or local television programs. The security industry is a source of fascination to many people, and you never know who is out in the audience who may contact you for a new project.

Volunteer to address local civic and business groups for luncheon and dinner presentations. If you are dynamic you will be remembered and called upon again, and eventually those appearances will lead to consulting assignments.

Run for a public office in your home town, city, or country, or volunteer to sit on some governmental committee or board. Contacts you make can only enhance your exposure as a professional consultant.

Direct Mailings

American Business Lists in Omaha, Nebraska, has lists of 10 million businesses in this country. The magazine they sell which lists the various businesses is an eye opener. Let's say you have an interest in conducting security surveys for various religious facilities (I do not know of any colleague who does that). According to this Nebraska firm, they have the names and addresses of 1,070 convents and monasteries. So one could obtain such a list and directly mail a personalized letter or a professionally prepared flyer, soliciting their business.

Probably direct mailings should be handled by professional marketing people who are working in your behalf because they know the ins and outs of that strategy. But it is something the individual consultant can do on his or her own.

Business Cards

Business cards for consultants must be of the highest quality paper, printing and layout. Again, this is a job for those who make a living providing business cards. The business card is your personal calling card as well as your professional card. A card can and does say a great deal about its giver. Do not ever give out a card that is marred or bent. Do not ever make a correction such as new phone number or address on a card. Do not use your card for making notes.

Promotional Sundries

Promotional items that bear the consultant's name, address, telephone number, and logo are restricted by nothing but your imagination. I have seen the following:

- calendars (pocket and wall)
- pens
- china cups
- rulers

Many of us feel ambivalent about such items, but do recognize that most people

FIGURE 5–1   *Example of a marketing brochure. (Reproduced by permission of Mark M. Warrington, CPP.)*

Taking A Business-Like And Creative Approach To Security And Safety Management

MANAGING RISK

All organizations face an array of security, safety, and other potential loss exposures.

Managers need to understand these threats and the options available to counter them. This provides a basis for deciding which protective measures and expenditures are justified in relation to the risks identified.

Inadequate security/safety can cause serious financial losses; incur liability; drain profits; damage morale; and cause loss of confidence by various communities.

Effective management of risks can help prevent problems and improve protection of people, property, information, and the environment. It can also help preserve the organization's ability to operate, and provide management peace-of-mind.

Warrington & Associates, Inc. draws on first-hand experience to help clients define effective strategies and to develop cost-effective solutions tailored to meet the specific needs of the customer's organization.

The professional consulting services offered by Warrington & Associates, Inc. are an effective way to evaluate needs and plan effective security and safety programs.

SERVICES

1. EVALUATION
- Security/safety needs assessment
- Risk analysis, vulnerability assessment
- Comprehensive security surveys
- Program performance audits

2. MANAGEMENT PLANNING
- Strategic master planning and program design
- Planning and design of integrated security systems
- Organizational development for safety and security staff
- Disaster recovery plans, emergency response programs

3. PROGRAM DEVELOPMENT
- Comprehensive security/safety program design
- Policy development, standard practices, procedures
- Program testing, validation, and implementation support
- Prevention programs (crime, loss, accident, violence)

4. TRAINING
- Training program design, train-the-trainer
- Management briefings and seminars
- Inservice training for professionals and other staff
- Employee awareness and self help programs

5. SPECIAL SERVICES
- Problem solving, countermeasures for special threats
- Crisis management support
- Executive protection, counter-terrorism
- Litigation prevention

OUR STRATEGY

- Exceed customers expectations
- Work closely with clients as partners
- Ensure work is consonant with the primary mission and core values of the client organization
- Stay flexible and responsive to the needs of the customer and project
- Operate with the highest standards of ethics and professionalism

· SERVING ·

CORPORATIONS

PUBLIC AND PRIVATE INSTITUTIONS

GOVERNMENTS AND PUBLIC AGENCIES

PROFESSIONALS

WARRINGTON & ASSOCIATES, INC.

FIGURE 5–1 *Continued.*

ART INTELLIGENCE

Art Intelligence is a quarterly newsletter published by Robert E. Spiel Associates, Inc.— A leading provider of security and investigative services to the fine art and rare collectible communities. This newsletter is dedicated to providing current information and protective strategies to help safeguard those communities.

Summer, 1994 Issue

RECOVERIES REMAIN RARER THAN FINE ART ITSELF—
Renoirs Recovered, Munch No Longer Missing, But What Of Picassos, Braques, And More?

In March this year, Thomas Tarpley, a 24-year-old wallpaper hanger from Atlanta, GA, was arrested after decorating his garage with more than $1 million worth of stolen artwork. Two Renoirs as well as ten other paintings by Corot, Glackens, and others were recovered. This quarter, we can also celebrate the return of Edvard Munch's *The Scream* to its home in Norway's National Museum. Yet these recoveries barely scratch the surface of the mountains of stolen artwork around the world that remain missing.

In the last 10 years, more than $5.5 billion worth of art has been reported stolen to the FBI; very little has been retrieved. After the theft earlier this year of a Picasso from the Richard Gray Gallery in Chicago, art security expert and former FBI Special Agent Robert Spiel expressed his frustration to ABC Television: "There are now so many stolen Picassos floating around that the thieves probably won't have any problem fencing [this one]." (Another Picasso stolen from the same Chicago gallery in 1985 is just one of the many artworks still missing.) Mr. Spiel went on to explain that, because Picasso was

Continued on page 3

COLLECTIBLE CAPERS

Thief with a Fetish Thwarted at Last ... Merrill Shepro of LaGrange, IL, has a fetish for collectibles ... other people's collectibles! Shepro was arrested by police last Fall while casing a home in Naperville, IL. Among the items taken in a string of burglaries

Continued on page 4

ABOUT OUR EDITOR

The editor of *Art Intelligence* and president of Robert E. Spiel Associates, Inc., is Bob Spiel. Bob dedicated most of his 20-year career as a Special Agent with the FBI, to the recovery of stolen fine art and rare collectibles, and to the prosecution of those engaged in the theft or forgery of these objects.

In 1988, Bob resigned his commission to establish a private-sector firm dedicated to the same goals and to develop protective strategies tailored to the unique characteristics of all collectors' items. Bob is a Certified Protection Professional, a Licensed Private Detective, and a director of the International Association of Professional Security Consultants.

ART APPROPRIATED

Art Buys in Cocaine Cash Cover-Up
The art world and the world of drug dealing are both international businesses in which a great deal of money changes hands very rapidly. A recent case involving two brothers readily illustrates how the drug trade is taking increasing advantage of this similarity by using legitimate art transactions to cover up illegitimate profits from drug trafficking.

Eric Wells of Austin, MN, who was identified as the leader of a major

cocaine distribution ring, is now serving a twelve-year sentence in federal prison. He was convicted last year for conspiring to distribute more than 300 pounds of cocaine, and for money laundering. Earlier this year, Wells' brother, Duane L. Graff, a nearby art dealer, came clean over his own role in Wells' drug money laundering operation. Graff admitted he helped Wells conceal profits from the drug business by accepting $40,000 in artwork as a so-called

Continued on page 2

Have a question for Spiel Associates?
Call Bob Spiel at 312-861-1313 or send a fax to 312-616-4215.

FIGURE 5–2   *Example of a newsletter. (Reproduced by permission of Robert E. Spiel Associates, Inc.)*

enjoy receiving gifts; and, if the promotional item is of sufficient quality, certainly no harm can come of it.

Authorship

Publishing articles can expose you to any market, primarily due to the never-ending need for articles in trade publications. Besides, people have a natural interest in and curiosity about the topic of crime.

Newsletters

Your own newsletter can be an effective marketing tool. They are not hard to write, particularly if it is only four pages and produced quarterly. The contents can be a distillation of what has been published in other periodicals, what's happening in the consultant's field of specialization, and be advisory in nature. The real value lies in the promotional impact it has on prospective clients. The author is seen as professional, authoritative, credible, current, and available!

Some newsletters are used for revenue purposes. The value I see, for the purpose of this writing, is the marketing aspects.

Pro Bono Work

The Latin term *pro bono* means "for the public good." In our society it means professional work done for some good cause without charging a fee—professional voluntary service on a specific assignment. For example, I served as the consultant, without charge, for an early Californian Franciscan Mission. Such service not only "gives back" in some measure, for all we receive in this life, but does have the possible result of being called upon for compensating work by someone who observed your free work.

Reference was made earlier in this chapter to a hypothetical consulting assignment in a hospital gift shop which could lead to expanded assignments. That very example could well be started as a *pro bono* effort.

Chapter 6

The Proposal and Contract

Every consulting assignment requires a consultant's proposal to provide such service. The proposal is usually in writing, typically submitted in response to a prospective client's request, commonly referred to in our industry as the request for proposal (RFP). The process follows a track like this:

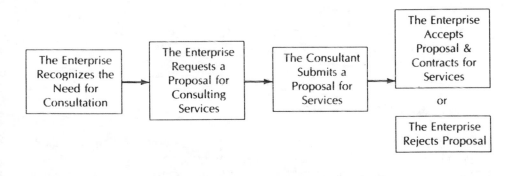

THE ENTERPRISE RECOGNIZES THE NEED FOR CONSULTATION

As I have indicated before, a corporate entity must be motivated to bring in outside expertise to assess a known concern and offer advice on how to solve the problem. That motivation must be of such a magnitude that it has senior management's attention and organizational priority.

For example, in a retail company the motivation could be that the recently calculated annual inventory reflects an extremely high shrinkage—with a disastrous impact on profitability. A healthcare administrator could be prompted by a recent sexual assault on a bedridden patient to review the security program. A security officer for a corporation could have arrested and assaulted a party, resulting in a punishing lawsuit against the organization, so that now management is anxious to avoid another similar experience. Whatever the type of enterprise or problem, consulting services appear to company managers to be their solution.

THE ENTERPRISE REQUESTS A PROPOSAL

Typically, the organization will delegate to a senior member the task of identifying qualified consultants and obtaining proposals for evaluation. Once consultants are identified, the request for a proposal is made. The request may be accomplished via a telephone conversation or during a preliminary meeting. Or, the request for the proposal may come in written format, from a simple letter to a lengthy formal request for proposal. The direction is usually clear: the prospective client wants a proposal that identifies the following:

1. What you will do
2. How you will do it
3. Who will do it
4. Where you will do it
5. When you will do it
6. How much you will charge to do it

These six points encompass what a proposal is all about.

THE CONSULTANT SUBMITS PROPOSAL FOR SERVICES

How a proposal is written directly affects the results. A poorly written and hastily prepared proposal may lose your prospective assignment, while a professionally prepared proposal may land you the job. Why? The proposal works as a preview of coming attractions; it provides a window through which the prospective client can see how you organize work, how you articulate and communicate, how you grasp problems and see connections that lead to probable solutions. Such conclusions, true or false, are indeed drawn from the presentation of your proposal.

The best way to demonstrate what a properly prepared proposal should look like is to use an actual proposal as a model. The following was submitted by my colleague, Robert O. Murphy, to a hospital whose name is changed for confidentiality:

PROPOSAL
to
BLUE MEMORIAL HOSPITAL

Security Audit Inc. proposes to conduct a study at Blue Memorial Hospital relating to external security considerations. The overall objective will be to answer the question, "What does the hospital do to provide a secure exterior environment and are these measures reasonable and sufficient to achieve their purposes?"

I. Scope
    The security audit will cover these facets:
    - Security measures presently utilized with respect to the parking lots and the new parking garage.
    - Efficiency of external security hardware now in use.
    - Security considerations involved in routing hospital visitors using the garage directly to the hospital's main entrance, rather than through the Professional Office Bldg.
    - Added security responsibility resulting from completion of the New Pavilion Wing.
    - Assessment of the need to devise arrangements limiting use of the hospital vending, dining, and gift facilities to those who have a valid reason to be in the hospital.
    - Study of the quality and extent of liaison between the hospital's Security Department and the Bluetown Police Dept.

II. Approach
    Exterior patrol schedules and practices of the Security Dept. will be reviewed. The effectiveness of current practices with respect to the parking lots and the new parking garage will be considered.

    Those external security devices presently utilized will be observed and their efficiency gauged. This will include exterior cameras and any other equipment presently in place on the exterior of the premises.

    The pedestrian traffic pattern from the new garage to the hospital will be studied from the security standpoint. Clearly, it is desirable that such traffic move directly to the hospital's main entrance when visitors are involved, rather than through the Professional Office Bldg. The latter route affords no opportunity for the identification or direction of visitors.

    When the New Pavilion Wing is completed, ninety-six beds will be added to the hospital's census. With this addition comes a commitment to provide commensurate security. Physical observation will be made and blueprints reviewed in an effort to suggest means whereby the exterior areas of the Pavilion might be adequately protected.

    A study will be made as to the need to devise arrangements to insure that those who come to the hospital have a valid reason for doing so. This constituency would include patients, visitors, staff members, employees, tradespeople, and suppliers. It does not include casual users of the hospital's vending, dining, or gift facilities, who otherwise have no reason to be in the hospital; nor does it include anyone whose purposes are clearly inimical to the best interests and proper functioning of the hospital.

    Police Services are essential in the operation of almost any hospital, and they are an important consideration here at Blue Memorial. Sufficient Security Department records will be reviewed to determine the extent of services afforded by the Bluetown Police Dept., and a determination will be made as to the quality of those services.

III. Resolution
    At the conclusion of the information-gathering phase, an analysis will be made of our findings and tentative recommendations prepared. Thereafter, these

recommendations will be discussed with the Vice President-Administration to ensure that the recommendations meet standards of reasonableness and feasibility.

To follow will be our written report containing the substance of our findings. It will be written without attribution but will be based on solid documentation developed during the study. The report will contain recommendations, as required. Two copies of the report will be produced by the release date.

IV.   Engagement Considerations and Limitations
The study will be conducted in a professional, low-key manner. It is understood that this review does not connote any dissatisfaction with the hospital's Security Department or its management. Rather, it is a positive effort to ensure that reasonable provision has been made to protect the hospital and all who come here.

V.   Project Organization and Security Audit Inc. Background
(*In this section is a short history of the consulting firm and a short biographical sketch of the principal consultant, Mr. Murphy, and a short biographical sketch of three other consultants.*)

Security Audit Inc. reserves the right to utilize the services of (*names of the other consultants*) only if the requirements of the project establish the need for such utilization.

VI.   Fees and Time Commitment
Our fee for this study will be based on our standard rates. We estimate that the cost of our services for this project will approximate $_____.

It is noted that charges are not assessed for travel time. Only time spent on-site or time utilized off-site in analysis or the preparation of written materials is charged.

We will bill in two installments for services, submitting the initial statement at the end of thirty days and the final statement when the report is delivered.

The dates for the project will be secured by agreement between the Hospital and Security Audit Inc. If the hospital desires that the project be completed by the end of December (this year) and approval of this proposal is forthcoming, every effort will be made to deliver the report within the desired time frame.

October 29, 19____

Blue Memorial Hospital administrators, who perceived the need for security consulting services in the form of an assessment now had in hand at least one proposal to provide such services. The proposal submitted by Murphy certainly informed the decision-makers in that hospital as to what his service would do, how he would do it, who would or could be involved in doing it, where it would be done, how much it would cost the hospital, and when the project could be completed.

THE ENTERPRISE ACCEPTS PROPOSAL AND CONTRACTS FOR SERVICES

The hospital favorably responded to Murphy's proposal with the following letter:

November 9, 19_____

Dear Bob:

I have reviewed your proposal in response to my request for a study at the hospital involving a number of specific concerns. Your proposal summarizes the areas that we are anxious to have audited, and I would like you to proceed as soon as possible.

The recent event involving the arrest of an individual who was on the patient floors posing as a visitor, has increased our need to devise arrangements to ensure that those who come into the hospital have a valid reason for doing so.

As I mentioned earlier, we would like the results of your study prior to the end of this year. It is my understanding that this timetable is acceptable.

I look forward to reviewing your findings and recommendations.

Sincerely,

Vice President for Administration

This letter not only represents the acceptance of the proposal but also serves as the contract for the consulting assignment. No other written documents, except the report of the assessment and invoice, are required in this relationship. And this is the norm in the independent security consulting field. More typically, the contract is in the form of a letter from the client who accepts the proposal, spells out conditions and expectations, and authorizes you to perform. The acceptance letter serves in every sense of the word as a contract. If you fail to perform, the client will not pay and a court of law would compare your performance to this contractual letter. If you do perform, and the client does not pay, again, the judicial system would look to the letter as the agreement between the two parties.

That is not to say that formally prepared and signed contracts are never used. Occasionally they may be required, and if so, the requirement derives from the client, not the consultant. Appendix A includes a consulting contract that serves as a model. Appendix B shows another example of a contract, taken from the *Protection of Assets* manual.

The Letter of Understanding

The above-cited contract in the form of a letter of acceptance of the consultant's proposal listed specific tasks to be undertaken. The acceptance letter from the hospital compliments Murphy's proposal in terms of understanding the conditions of the business relationship. Sometimes, as in a letter written by a client after a proposal meeting, the letter is the only written instrument that spells out the venture, and it is best described as a *letter of understanding*. Such a letter, as does a proposal, spells out the who, what, where, how, when, and how much. There are times, too, when the letter of understanding is initiated by the consultant. Following is a sample letter of understanding I directed to the president of an over-the-road freight carrier:

February 19, 19_____
    Dear Mr. Henderson:
    This correspondence constitutes a LETTER OF UNDERSTANDING regarding the upcoming Security Survey I will conduct at your facility. Commencing February 25, 19XX, I will embark upon an assessment of your facility, the scope of which will include but not necessarily be limited to the physical security and controls, policies, and procedures as they impact on security, security personnel and practices, claims, and management/supervisory involvement. This survey will include regular as well as evening hours of operation.
    Following my on-site inspection and review, I will prepare and submit to you a written report outlining my observations, along with recommendations to correct or modify as appropriate.

    My fee is $_____ ($_____ per hour for an 8-hour day) per day

plus actual expenses, except mileage which is billed at _____¢ per mile. I anticipate no more than four (4) days' work; and the final invoice will reflect actual hours committed to the task. Invoice will be presented along with two bound copies of the report, and payment for services will be made upon receipt of reports and invoice.
    I plan to arrive at your office at 1:00 pm, February 25th, would like to start right off by meeting with your financial vice president, Mr. _____.
    I look forward to this effort and our meeting on February 25th. Until then, I remain,

                    Sincerely,
                    Charles A. Sennewald, CPP

I had offered a verbal proposal, and the firm's president was satisfied and asked me to proceed with the project. But I did not want to undertake that project (or any project) without some form of contract or written agreement. I chose not to ask company personnel to prepare the letter of agreement; I saw that as my chore. My letter, then, spelled out the required who, what, where, how, when, and how much and hence served as our contract.

The consultant must have some form of written documentation or contract, be it a letter of proposal acceptance, a written agreement, or a letter of understanding (initiated by either party) to refer back to in the event of any downstream misunderstanding or disagreement as to the project.

Not all consulting assignments are for one specific project. Some consulting relationships span an ongoing period of time, often referred to as a *retainer basis.* Most retainer relationships are for an agreed-upon minimum fee, usually represented in the form of a minimum number of hours per month with compensation for those number of hours, even if no work is performed. Example: a consultant can agree to service a company for one half-day per month (4 hours) at $150 per hour, or $600 a month. The client may require service that entails less than that much time, yet the consultant is paid for the four hours. If the hours exceed the minimum, however, the consultant will be compensated for all hours worked. This agreement, too, must be evidenced in writing.

Similarly, an ongoing relationship can exist without an actual retainer agreement, and with no fixed times or fees. Normally that kind of relationship must also be outlined in some form of writing, if for no other reason than to avoid any future misunderstanding.

Following is a letter of understanding I sent to a new client whom I subsequently served for several years:

February 20, 19_____

Dear Mr. Hall:

This letter constitutes a LETTER OF UNDERSTANDING regarding our working relationship and compensation for services rendered and expenses incurred:

1. We are not in a contractual or retainer relationship; thus, services requested or rendered may be terminated at any time without advance or formal notification.
2. My consultation fee is $XXX.XX per hour.
3. All travel time is billable.
4. All "back office" work is billed at the same hourly rate, with the exception of phone conferences. There will be no charge for that service.
5. Expenses: actual only. Typically they include first-class air transportation, hotel accommodations, meals, auto rental, long distance phone calls, and use of my personal auto at _____¢ per mile.
6. Billing is on the first day of each month.

Should you have any questions regarding this letter, please don't hesitate to call.

I look forward to being of service. Until our next meeting on March 11th, I remain,

Sincerely,
Charles A. Sennewald, CMC, CPP

It should be noted that, had there been an ongoing retainer arrangement, the terms and conditions would easily have been enumerated in the letter of understanding.

Confidentiality Contracts

Some clients may require the consultant to sign an agreement of confidentiality or *nondisclosure agreement*, wherein the consultant agrees not to use or disclose information obtained from the client to competitors or anyone else not privy to the organization's proprietary data. For an example of a nondisclosure agreement, see Appendix C. This is a reasonable expectation and requirement. Regardless of any such written promise, however, the confidentiality of information should be the unwritten guideline and philosophy of every responsible and professional security consultant.

A Word of Caution About Proposals

There are occasions when a prospective client sends out RFPs when they already know who will get the consulting assignment. This is done because there's a requirement that it be put out to bid or there is the need, for whatever reason, to give the appearance that the process was competitive. I have been a victim of this and there is really not much one can do other than check around with other consultants to see what information exists about this upcoming project and act accordingly.

Another risk lies in detailed proposals being used as a guide or blueprint for someone else to follow, i.e., you have laid out a consulting program to solve their problem and the prospective client has its own security executive follow your outline.

These "bumps in the road" need not discourage the new consultant. Submitting proposals is a way of life in this business. It is just better to be forewarned and be wary as to how much time and detail you invest in a given proposal.

Chapter 7

The Survey

The consultant's task is usually that of assessing a client's existing security situation and recommending positive change. Change is not inevitable; some conditions may not, in the consultant's opinion, warrant change. But typically, some modifications to the existing company's strategy or program are required. Recommended changes are based on the consultant's evaluation of existing conditions. That evaluation is inherently judgmental.

The primary vehicle used in a security assessment is the survey. The survey is the process whereby one gathers data that reflects the who, what, how, where, when, and why of the client's existing operation. The survey is the fact-finding process. The assessment is the final appraisal, the conclusion drawn from those facts and recommendations for improvement.

The breadth and depth of an initial survey and the resulting assessment are limited by the scope of the work, which must be determined at the outset of the consulting assignment. Sometimes the client has predetermined the exact scope of the work; other times, the consultant must provide guidance or otherwise assist the client in defining the scope of the work. The retailer in Chapter 3 who wanted me to assess only the merchandise distribution system was defining a narrow scope of work. That scope was determined prior to contacting me for discussion. The scope of work in this project was narrow indeed! Imagine: it *excluded* almost everything one associates with retail security, such as shoplifting detection policies and procedures, shoplifting detection training, documentation, and recordation. And it excluded dishonest employee investigation policies and procedures, interrogation, and interviewing practices. But the well-defined scope of the work—to assess the company's policies and procedures pertaining to the receiving, distribution, and transfer of merchandise from a security perspective, was a logical objective. And the consulting project proceeded efficiently because the scope of the project allowed for a methodical plan of attack, because the direction was defined.

Then again, I have met with a chief executive officer (CEO) who had decided he wanted a security survey but did not understand what that could entail. I could not commence the project until I had determined what he wanted and what he did not want—the scope of the work. Because it was clear to me that he had not thought through his options, I led the CEO through the following conversation:

CEO:	We've experienced significant losses despite a rather expensive security program and need you to simply do what you must to give us some guidance on tightening up and maximizing our present security expend- itures.
Consultant:	You have another facility across the state line. Do you want me to include that in my survey?
CEO:	Oh no. Just this site. We have a different situation over there. What you see and do here we can apply there, so please don't bother with them.
Consultant:	I note you're using a contract security service. Are you interested in the possibility of setting up a proprietary force?
CEO:	No. In fact, don't worry about changing the guard force. For our own reasons we must continue with that service. With that in mind, look at that force in terms of the quality of people they're sending us, the training they receive, the duties they perform, and whether they are doing what they should be doing. You know—are we getting our money's worth?
Consultant:	Who supervises these security officers?
CEO:	That's a problem area. I know who is supposed to oversee the guards and their work, but I suspect there's some competition there [among my own staff], to the detriment of the program.
Consultant:	All right, so you want an assessment of the existing security staff and their function and supervision. And as you indicated earlier, you want me to look at the physical aspects of security, here at this main site. That would include access control, alarm systems, fencing and other barriers, lighting, the key control system, access to the computer room, and—
CEO:	Please do not include the computer operation in your work. We recently had a computer expert out here and he's already given us direction in that area, so anything you do there would be redundant.

Note how this brief conversation refined and defined the scope of the project and excluded areas that, had they not been identified, would have wasted time and expense to the dissatisfaction of the client. So, it is incumbent upon the consultant to ensure that the expectations of the client are clarified.

Yet, as careful as one may be in defining this scope of the work, problems invariably surface. Security Consultant James Broder and I collaborated on a major hospital assignment. We had clearly defined the scope of the work. Some days into the project we discovered, to our amazement, the hospital had two off-site clinics, both some miles away from the main hospital campus. We had no choice but to add those sites to our survey—additional work not included in our estimate.

THE PRELIMINARY SURVEY

The above example of dialogue between the consultant and client is a part of what is called the preliminary survey. The preliminary survey may consist of four parts:

initial meeting with management
tour of the facility
meetings with key managerial personnel
final meeting with management to agree upon scope of the work

These four steps are not mandatory, but rather are ideal. Depending on many circumstances, the entire preliminary survey may be restricted to the initial meeting with management. That initial meeting might include a brief facility tour; later, key personnel could be invited to sit in and answer questions posed by the consultant; this way, the scope of the work gets finalized before that one meeting adjourns.

Naturally, this truncated version of the preliminary survey cannot reveal as much information as would the four separate steps. The client's budget for the consulting assignment may constrain preliminary activities to a single management meeting. Yet, if the project involves aspects that are relatively unfamiliar to the consultant, the four steps might be essential.

Let us examine more closely the four phases of the preliminary survey.

Step 1: Initial Meeting with Management

This initial meeting gives managers their first opportunity to articulate their real concerns about security and to spell out what their expectations are. This initial meeting also catalyzes the development of the consulting game plan. Part of any consulting strategy requires the complete cooperation of all members of the management team. To achieve that kind of organizational cooperation, the chairperson or chief executive officer should affix his or her signature to a management memorandum that:

1. announces the company's decision and commitment to undertake the consulting relationship
2. asks every executive for complete cooperation with and assistance to the consultant(s)
3. authorizes the release or divulgence of company records and information not normally shared with others
4. introduces the consultant by name, including a brief biographical sketch

Another decision at this initial meeting is the appointment of a manager to work with the consultant. This person schedules appointments, makes introductions, and assists the consultant in every way possible, "opening doors" to expedite the consultant's work. Finally, the timetable for the process is set. This may include the setting of a midpoint when senior management may expect a progress briefing by the consultant, as well as the due date for completion of the project and report.

Step 2: Tour of the Facility

If you are contemplating remodeling a building, you should see the building in its entirety as it currently exists. And so it is with the consultant who is about to survey a regional shopping center or major hotel. You need to walk through the property for orientation, for the magnitude of the site, and for general impressions regarding the demographics and clientele. The totality of that experience makes for an important frame of reference during subsequent work on the project. For example, if you note graffiti on the walls of the building, you might later question the frequency and routing of patrols, the presence or absence of lighting, or the required reports by patrolling officers.

Step 3: Select Meetings with Key Managerial Personnel

Discussions with key managerial personnel are critical to the consulting process for two reasons:

1. To allow managers to express their concerns about security in the corporation, from their own perspective, and for whatever benefit those observations may have in and of themselves.
2. To include managers in the consulting process so that *they have ownership* in some measure in the outcome of the consultation. If they are not included in the interviewing, if the consultant fails to elicit their input, they tend to distance themselves from the program and the final recommendations. They may be more likely to criticize the changes that occur.

Note the word *key* managerial personnel. Every manager considers herself or himself "key," right? Thus, the more people included, the more ownership you will have in your work product. Realistically, you may not reach them all. But do what you can.

Step 4: Final Meeting with Management to Agree upon Scope of the Work

This is the pouring of concrete regarding the objectives and scope of the consulting assignment. If indeed this fourth step occurs, as such, it provides an excellent opportunity for the consultant to share with senior management some initial impressions and observations. This, too, is the time to retrace the consulting strategy and timetable.

THE SURVEY ITSELF

The survey is no more nor less than an information-gathering, fact-finding process. Such process is accomplished in three ways:

1. *interviewing*: talking with knowledgeable people to gather information via the spoken word
2. *observation*: physical viewing of physical features such as fences, lights, officers' uniforms, and locking systems to gather information via the power of visual observation
3. *research*: examining records, policies, files, organizational charts, and job descriptions to gather information via the written word

All three of these fact-finding processes may apply to one problem. Take this hypothetical question: How does a company's access control program work on Sundays and holidays? To answer that question the consultant would interview security officers who work on Sundays and holidays and employees who enter the facility on those days; the consultant would examine the entry-door used as well as the remote control or card reader, and view the CCTV camera and monitor used to surveil that access point; and review the hard-copy reports generated on those days as well as the policy and procedure manual that spells out what should happen. The end result of that fact-gathering process will suggest to the consultant what change or modification is appropriate, if any.

Other surveys may require but one fact-gathering process, such as interviewing security officers as to their understanding of the department's mission (in those cases where there is no printed mission statement). Whatever the scope of the work, the survey will focus on four component parts of a security program. The sum total of these four component parts equals the security program:

$$
\left.\begin{array}{l}
\text{Policy} \\
\text{Procedure} \\
\text{Physical plant/equipment/hardware} \\
\text{Personnel}
\end{array}\right\} = \text{Protection program}
$$

So that any problems in the security program must exist within one or more of the component parts:

$$
\left.\begin{array}{l}
\text{Policy failure} \\
\text{Procedural failure} \\
\text{Physical plant/equipment deficiency} \\
\text{Personnel shortage or failures}
\end{array}\right\} = \text{Program problems}
$$

In the format of an equation it would look like this:

$$p + p + p + p = Pp \quad \text{(viable Protection program)}$$

or

 $+ p + p + p =$ (Protection program in trouble)

The $p-$ in the above equation represents a shortcoming, failure, or deficiency that mitigates against a balanced and healthy program. These component parts allow us to form compartments for a closer scrutiny of the consulting process. Let us examine these parts.

First P is POLICY

The key word in understanding Policy is *what*. Policy represents *what* management wants, *what* management expects. For example, the policy in one retail firm is to detect, apprehend, and prosecute every shoplifter. That is the policy. Now, if company leaders state that policy yet release some shoplifters for various reasons, the inconsistency of practice against policy could be the source of a significant litigation. If it is deemed reasonable to release some shoplifters due to factors of health or age or the amount of the theft, then those exceptions should be reflected in the policy. Other policy areas could include:

1. What is the policy regarding escorting female employees to their cars in the parking lot after dark?
2. What is the policy regarding employees possessing alcoholic beverages or drugs on the company premises?
3. What is the policy for coping with an employee who refuses to be interviewed by a security investigator regarding missing supplies?
4. What is the policy regarding the arming of security officers?
5. What is the policy regarding disciplinary action for an example, against an employee with twenty-five years service who has been detected in a $5 theft?

Policy is fundamental to security. If a company has an internal theft problem and has no consistent stand on the consequences of being caught stealing, the internal theft problem cannot effectively be addressed, let alone reduced.

Second P is PROCEDURE

The key word in understanding Procedure is *how*. Procedure represents *how* management wants things done. For example, a retail firm's policy may be to detect, apprehend, and prosecute shoplifters. But they do not want the apprehending security agent to use excessive force—the application of only a reasonable level of force to restrain the offender until the police arrive is permissible. That is *how* management wants apprehensions to be conducted.

Procedures usually are outlined in written format, but sometimes you will find procedures reflected in custom and practice.

The consultant will focus on procedures essential to the scope of the work. If, for example, the scope is on the problems of litigation and public complaint concerning the treatment (or alleged treatment) of shoplifters, the preservation of evidence in defense of possible lawsuits, and the deportment of the shoplifting security agents, the consultant would probably scrutinize the following procedures:

- recruiting for shoplifting agents
- interviewing shoplifting agent candidates
- verifying candidates' work history and references
- ensuring that potential employees do not have a propensity for or history of violence
- training for shoplifting security agents
- monitoring and reviewing security agents' work
- preserving shoplifting evidence
- monitoring the status of court cases for continued preservation of evidence; freedom to return evidence to stock because case has been closed

When operating procedures are unclear or undocumented, or contrary to industry custom and practice, or indeed are illegal or wasteful, the consultant will recommend correction and documentation in the form of written guidelines or an operating procedural manual.

Third P is for PHYSICAL PLANT AND EQUIPMENT

Rare would be the security survey that does not examine the physical aspects of protection. This component part of the security program could include:

- the building configuration, including doors, windows, roof access, and subterranean access
- access controls
- fencing
- lighting
- key controls and lock hardware
- CCTV
- alarm systems
- communication system
- patrol supervisory systems
- patrol vehicles
- uniforms

Each of these subcategories prompts a host of questions and concerns that would necessarily be included in the survey. Take as an example, fences:

1. Does the fence completely enclose the property when the gates are closed?
2. Does the fence meet industry standards?
3. Does the fence have protective topping? Should it?
4. Is there evidence the fence has been scaled?

5. Can the fenceline be penetrated through holes in the fencing itself, or can it be easily crawled under?
6. When the gates are secured, is there still room to slip through and enter the property?
7. Are there trees next to the fence that would facilitate climbing over the fence?
8. Is the fenceline cleared of shrubs, weeds, or other obstructions that would permit the hiding of persons or materials?
9. Can vehicles drive up to the fenceline?
10. Is lighting required along the fence?
11. If buildings constitute part of the perimeter, are windows secured so that penetration by persons or materials is restricted?
12. If buildings constitute part of the perimeter and conjoin the perimeter fence or wall, do they form a vulnerable point in the protective enclosure?
13. Are the gates secured with padlocks to which keys can be purchased at the local hardware store? Who controls keys and where are they kept?

As the consultant moves through her or his survey of the physical plant, noting the answers to these concerns, any failures, omissions, and needed corrections will be duly noted and subsequently reflected in the final report. (For a more comprehensive example of how to prepare and conduct a security survey, see Appendix D).

Fourth P is PERSONNEL

Because security is every employee's responsibility, this category comprises all personnel—not just security employees. Such concerns as hiring, screening and selection practices, new employee induction/orientation programs, employee participation in safety/security committees, and general loss-prevention awareness programs, *or their absence*, are of interest to the consultant.

Moreover, the individual officer's perceptions of role and mission, his or her impression of the boss's expectations, idiosyncratic likes and dislikes, can be revealed through the interview. Questions you could ask include:

1. Why are you in security work?
2. Where do you go from here?
3. What do you like most about your job?
4. What do you like least about your job? Why?
5. What is the mission of this security department?
6. If you could make changes in how the security department goes about its task, what would you change?
7. What does security do that you consider a waste of time? Why?
8. What is security not doing that it should?
9. Does the director of security know what you do? How do you know? Do you think she/he cares?

10. Do you have the tools to do what is expected of you? If not, what do you need?
11. What kind of training did you receive when you first came here? Was it sufficient?
12. Do you receive any ongoing training?
13. What kind of training do you think you need?
14. Do you feel security is respected in this company?
15. When were you last evaluated or told how you rated against your peers?
16. Do you feel free to make suggestions?

A company that seeks to reduce losses and increase profitability must rely, in some measure, on the goodwill of its employees. Employees, including security people, who do not understand or share the firm's goals tend to impede progress toward such goals. Conversely, the staff that identifies with management goals, the employee who sees those goals as his or her own, tends to be supportive of the procedures and policies toward the enterprise's objectives. If they see themselves as part of the process and can measure their growth and recognition along with the firm's, then an attack against the company is an attack against them.

And after all, employees breathe life into policy and procedure and make physical safeguards function or fail. So the consultant's survey delves into this component— an arena frequently ignored by management.

Now the consultant has completed the initial gathering of factual information by way of the survey. Interviewing, observing, and researching have brought data to enable the security consultant to inform, judge, evaluate, and recommend in the form of the final report.

Chapter 8

The Consultant's Report

Whereas the survey is the means to identify the client's existing condition and needs, the consultant's *report* is the end, the work product itself. The report, which reflects the consultant's findings and recommendations, is what consulting is all about. Everything preceding the report is merely incidental in contrast to the ultimate value of the finished report. Consequently, in the aftermath of this document, the fortunes of the consultant rise or fall. An experienced, bright consultant who produces a poor report probably will not last long as a consultant. Conversely, the man or woman who produces a quality report will earn an established reputation and small distractions, such as personality traits, will be overlooked by prospective clients because of the reputation for quality work. And is this not how it should be? How else can one measure or grade a consultant's work? The quality of the consultant's work equals the quality of the final report.

COMPONENTS OF THE REPORT

The report typically is presented in a bound-booklet format. The cover may be purchased from a stationery store. As a matter of style and practice I like to use the client's logo on the cover and a clear acetate over that to give the booklet a glossy appearance (see Figure 8–1). The first page inside the heavy cover is a cover letter or title page, followed by the table of contents (see Figures 8–2 and 8–3). Figure 8–3 is an actual table of contents from a 43-page report on the survey of a major hospital. Note how the work is divided and presented in seven major categories:

executive summary

introduction

scope

findings

conclusions

recommendations

attachments

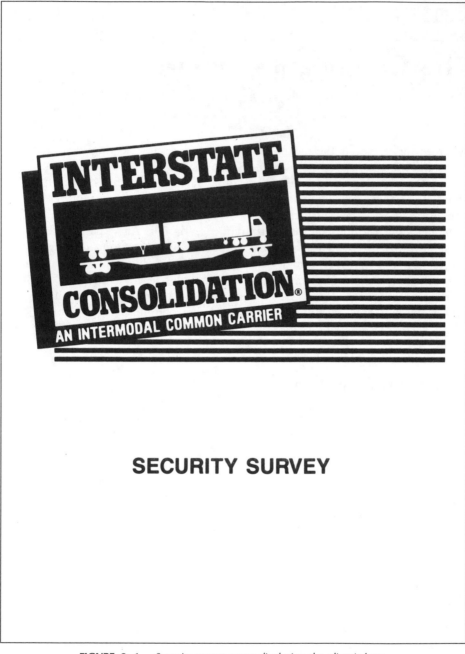

FIGURE 8–1   *Security report cover displaying the client's logo.*

CONFIDENTIAL

SECURITY SURVEY

INTERSTATE CONSOLIDATION SERVICE, INC.

March 1, 1995

Conducted by:

Charles A. Sennewald, CMC, CPP
Charles A. Sennewald & Associates
28004 Lake Meadow Drive
Escondido, California 92026
619-749-7527

FIGURE 8–2 *Typical title page for a security report.*

TABLE OF CONTENTS

FIGURE 8–3   *Table of contents from an actual security report.*

The breakdown of these components of the report represents the logical division of the overall effort and the consultant's findings. Such division in the report format makes the work more comprehensible for the client. Let us examine each of these categories for content:

The Executive Summary

A standard communication technique in management is to condense and highlight the contents of the report itself. Key, salient points highlight this abbreviated version of the report, which provides the busy executive with an overview of the project. Following is the complete executive summary of the above-listed hospital report:

The field portion of this survey was conducted in May and June, 19____. The main purpose of the survey was to identify and evaluate security-related risk and the protection of hospital personnel, resources, and assets from the threat of internal and external criminal exposure. A secondary purpose was to review the Hospital Security Department's practices as they relate to and impact upon all departments of the Hospital, on all shifts.

Interviews of senior executives, administrative personnel, department managers, uniformed security officers, and other hospital personnel were conducted. Emphasis was focused on the main building complex; selected off-site locations (clinics and the warehouse complex) were also inspected. Hospital policies and procedures which addressed security and the protection of assets were reviewed and analyzed.

The findings of the survey team were generally positive. Most significant was the absence of recent, serious crime on or near the Hospital.

Some of the major areas audited during the survey that produced items requiring management's attention were as follows:

- The Hospital needs to establish and publish a comprehensive security policy with procedural guidelines to improve the effectiveness of the security operations.
- Background investigations can be accomplished more quickly and cost-effectively if done in-house.
- The Security Department is understaffed. Officers need more formalized supervision and training.
- Controls need to be implemented (they are already established) to further reduce the opportunity for employee pilferage and theft. The employee and visitor identification badge system used to control the flow of people is excellent.
- Parking lots are well protected and, for the most part, adequately lighted and frequently patrolled by uniform security officers, both day and night. This combination is undoubtedly responsible for the low level of security-related incidents on the streets and in the parking lots at and near the Hospital.
- Lock and key control needs to be formalized with a new written policy and procedural guidelines that address current practices for buildings both on- and off-site.
- Security, special purpose alarms, closed circuit TV cameras, and monitors need to

be consolidated and centralized in a dedicated, client-owned and operated, central alarm monitoring station. Installed security hardware should be programmed to complement other aspects of the security program.

- Property control procedures (with the exception of the Engineering Department) were found to be functional and, with minor adjustment, can be improved to further reduce opportunity for theft.

Security at the Hospital historically has operated in a reactive mode. We found evidence that suggests a desire by management to shift to a proactive security mode.

The full report runs for forty-three pages, yet the summary does provide the reader with meaningful insight into the project, does it not? In fact, if the balance of the report was unavailable, would just the points reflected in this summary provide direction for change?

The Introduction

The introduction is a one-paragraph statement explaining who authorized the consulting project, that is:

This survey and report were authorized by Ms. Constance Koskovich, Vice President Administration, Petersburg Hospital Medical Center (PHMC).

It also spells out the purpose of the consulting project, that is:

The primary purpose of the survey was to identify and evaluate security-related risk and the protection of the institution's personnel, resources, and assets from the threat of internal and external criminal exposure. A secondary purpose was to review the hospital security department's practices as they relate to and impact on the institution as a whole.

The introduction, then, really is more or less a recapitulation of the project's charter—the contract or agreement letter.

The Scope

Scope, in the context of the final report, refers to the range of employees interviewed, the physical locations included in the survey, and the source documents reviewed. For example, under the category *employees interviewed* you might write:

The survey consisted of interviews with senior executives, administrative personnel, department managers, uniformed security officers, and other personnel employed in various departments of the hospital.

Under documents reviewed:

Some of the documents made available for our review and analysis were:

- security incident reports
- administrative policy manual
- security job descriptions
- employee handbook
- I.D. badge policy and procedures.

This category reviews the data you collected through the interviewing, observing, and researching of the *survey*.

The Findings

The findings portion of the security report reflects the *existing conditions as revealed through the survey*. These conditions may be satisfactory or not. Many times, the condition speaks for itself; once such a condition is highlighted by the findings. This kind of glaring problem is reflected in the findings of the hospital security department's procedures, as reflected in the report:

C. Procedures

The security procedures we found to exist were fragmented, poorly written, and outdated. A comprehensive Security Policy and Procedures Manual does not exist. There are no written post orders to which a security officer might refer for guidance in the event of a questionable situation or an emergency. The Director of Safety and Security regards the necessity for developing written procedures and posted orders as a high priority.

An example of a serious procedural situation that must be avoided in the future is the manner in which security officers make arrests. We were advised of a situation where two Petersburg security officers pursued a reported thief beyond hospital grounds, made an arrest, and handcuffed the prisoner; they returned him to the hospital before calling the municipal police. The legality of the arrest was questionable. The crime reportedly was a misdemeanor, not committed in the presence of the person making the arrest as required by law.

In the absence of procedural guidelines and training concerning arrests and the proper methods of handling similar situations, judgment errors such as the one described could recur. Such errors expose the hospital to not only embarrassment but civil litigation..

Note how the report only *reports* the condition; this findings category does not pursue the obvious solutions. The recommendations section of the report will offer solutions to this deficiency. This sample consultant's report includes sixteen sections and numerous subsections under findings. The procedures section just extracted came from a subsection under the topic *security organization*. And so it is with every project. The consultant must divide the work logically through the sections of survey and again when orally presenting the finished product to the client.

Look again at the table of contents for the hospital report. Not only is the work logically organized, but contents are paginated for easy referencing for a given subject or area of concern. That is, parking lots are addressed on page twelve:

6. Parking lots

There are six parking lots located in, near, or adjacent to the main building complex at PHMC. All of the lots are protected by barrier fencing and gates that are sufficiently high (up to 8 feet) to discourage climbing. The only parking lots open 24 hours per day are lots #1 and #3. Parking lot #1 is located inside the main building complex. This lot was observed to be frequently patrolled by uniformed security officers, both day and night. Lot #3, where the majority of evening and night employees park, is provided with the continuous presence of a security officer. Lot #5, also used for employee parking in the evening, is closed at midnight and on weekends. It is frequently patrolled during the hours of darkness.

Employees on the night shifts stated that the physical presence of security officers and the K-9 patrol gave them a sense of well-being when leaving the hospital en route to their cars. One nurse stated that, at first glance, the hospital might look like an armed camp, but she felt the consensus of opinion of night employees was that security was responsible for the low level of criminal incidents. She stated this was especially significant in comparison to other hospitals with which she was familiar..

Not all findings in the survey reflect deficient or inadequate conditions. The findings reflect, objectively, all security-related conditions, good as well as bad—because in reality, more things are being done correctly than incorrectly. Hence, part of the consultant's findings support the existing program and tend to encourage management to continue in those areas which are on-track—and then to correct those areas that fail to meet the desired standard.

The Conclusions

This optional section may be omitted from the report without detracting from a report's professionalism. When included, it serves as a summation or retrospective overview of the survey's findings. Following are the conclusions offered in the sample hospital report:

The security program at this hospital is best described as suffering from growing pains. The program in place today is seen as a developmental process which has occurred over a period of years. Procedures, hardware, and staffing were established and implemented on an "as needed" basis, that is, to solve perceived problems as they arose.

Little thought was given to long-range planning or the establishment of a solid foundation upon which to build an effective security organization. Notwithstanding, the security program that exists today has effectively prevented any major criminal incident common to other hospitals in this area.

There is also evidence to suggest that management now desires to make a dramatic shift in emphasis from a reactive to a proactive security mode. This survey is one example of management's interest in identifying problems—past, present, and future, that could adversely affect the institution. Implementation of the recommendations, which follow, will be another.

The Recommendations

This is truly the heart of the report. Certainly managers want to know what is being done correctly and what needs to be changed especially what the consultant recommends as the fix or cure.

Recommendations for change can have monumental consequences throughout the organization. Imagine the impact on a retailer who is experiencing high inventory shortages when a consultant recommends a full interim physical inventory. Inventories are not only financially costly, but they generally disrupt the normal flow and operation of the business itself. Or, imagine the impact if a consultant recommends that employees detected in acts of theft and fraud against the employer be processed through the criminal justice system. Prior to the consultant's survey and recommendation, no employee had ever been prosecuted, only terminated. Certainly the consequences of that strategical change in the organization's policies and procedures could send some ripples through the ranks. So, the consultant's recommendations must be well-conceived, prudent, and reasonable, based on sound evidence. The cure should not hurt worse than the illness. Solutions should be cost-effective and operationally feasible.

Each recommendation must be numerically identified for reference. This identity of a recommendation is most important, because not all recommendations will be implemented or acted upon immediately. The recommendation coding works this way:

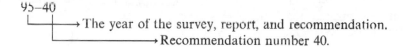

Some recommendations may be shelved for the next budget period and some may be controversial enough to be shelved indefinitely. Recommendations must be as succinct as possible. And they should be presented in the same sequence as the findings (as reflected in the table of contents). For example, in the sample model report the first area addressed in the *findings* was General, followed by Policy. The first recommendation was:

95–1 Develop and publish a Security and Loss Prevention Policy Statement. The statement should define the protection of hospital property as a basic management responsibility.

95–2 Plans to revise the Employee Handbook should include rewriting the statement on page 23 entitled "Safety and Security." Change the paragraph regarding security to read as follows:

The purpose of these officers is to maintain a level of safety and security for the protection of our employees, patients, and visitors, *to the extent reasonably possible*, as well as to prevent damage to or theft of hospital supplies, equipment, and property.

Other selected recommendations include:

95–14 The Director of Safety and Security should be afforded the opportunity of attending a security-related training program as soon as practically possible. We recommend The Protection of Assets course, presented by the American Society for Industrial Security.

Training seminars presented in conjunction with the International Association of Hospital Security Administrators should be attended by as many senior members of the security department as is practical.

95–23 Redesign and simplify the Security Department's Incident Report Form (see suggested form attached).

95–40 The CCTV camera monitoring the emergency room parking lot should have pan, tilt, and zoom capability. Presently it only pans and cannot be stopped.

95–42 Exterior telephones, particularly those located in the parking lots, should be incorporated into the emergency notification system presently in use with the panic button alarms.

All exterior telephones should be conspicuously identified—painted bright red or orange in color, equipped with night lights, and marked "For emergency use only."

The Attachments

It is not uncommon for a consultant to include attachments that support the report. The hospital model report included attachments such as a new security department organizational chart, a suggested simplified security incident report form, and a suggested policy statement.

If there are no attachments, then this section need not be included in the report.

AN ALTERNATIVE REPORT STRATEGY

Another report format that I have used when a report does not exceed two dozen pages deletes the executive summary and condenses the introduction, scope, and table of contents into one page. Experience shows that an executive summary is

CRIME AND LOSS REDUCTION   (619) 749-7527

CHARLES A. SENNEWALD & ASSOCIATES
SECURITY MANAGEMENT CONSULTING

This report reflects the findings and recommendations of a
security survey of the American University Bookstore's operation
conducted on August 7-9, 1995.

The objective of such survey was to assess existing conditions
and practices that directly or indirectly impact on inventory
shortages and, as a consequence, make cost-effective recommendations
to improve the shortage performance.

The survey focused on nine areas, which are:

1. General Inventory Shortage Control
2. The "Security Department"
3. Premises & Equipment
4. General Procedures
5. Documents and Forms
6. Human Resources Management
7. Shipping and Receiving
8. The Cashiering Operation
9. Security Programs

The nine areas are hereinafter referred to as AREAS OF CONCERN.
Under each AREA OF CONCERN is a listing of specific Observations,
immediately followed by the Consultant's Recommendation.
Recommendations are numbered for ease in referencing.

28004 LAKE MEADOW DRIVE, ESCONDIDO, CALIFORNIA 92026

FIGURE 8–4   *Condensed introduction and scope page for the shorter Observations and Recommendations report.*

unnecessary in short reports or when an ongoing dialogue with senior executives
has kept them aware of the bulk of the consultant's work. Figure 8–4 represents
this condensed version, which immediately precedes the actual findings and
recommendations (Figure 8-5).

```
OBSERVATION:            The thrust of the security effort is in the
                        detection of shoplifters, rather than the
                        prevention of loss, loss caused by all sources.

RECOMMENDATION #8:      Shift from a detection program to a prevention
                        program.  Consider a mix of plainclothes and
                        visible security, along the lines of the campus
                        patrol.

OBSERVATION:            Security personnel have been utilized only
                        during the hours the store is open.

RECOMMENDATION #9:      Expand the coverage to include all hours the
                        building is occupied by employees.

OBSERVATION:            The present Security Manual is deficient in the
                        areas of employee dishonesty, i.e., the who,
                        what, how, when employees may be challenged or
                        interviewed and the necessary documentation of
                        same.

RECOMMENDATION #10:     Based on written policy, expand the manual and
                        train accordingly.

OBSERVATION:            Because the emphasis has been on detection,
                        there's been no structured approach to the
                        other facets of protection, such as premises or
                        procedural security.

RECOMMENDATION #11:     Develop a checklist of non-detection duties
                        expected of a security agent.

OBSERVATION:            Training of security agents has been primarily
                        self-teaching and on-the-job, supplemented by
                        some instruction from the University Police.
                        This does not meet standards of practice.

RECOMMENDATION #12:     At Least once a year conduct a one-day training
                        program in retail security with professionals
                        in the business (who may be very reasonable in
                        their fees for such service), e.g., National
                        Drug Stores has an area security supervisor who
                        might lecture for an hour or so, etc.  Document
                        such training and ensure the personnel file of
                        each security employee reflects same.

                        AREA OF CONCERN #3

                        PREMISES & EQUIPMENT

OBSERVATION:            The copy center personnel have access to the
                        store's inventory with no controls.  In fact,
                        such employees are required to walk through the
                        stock area at the close of the day, after stock
                        and shipping & receiving personnel have left
                        for the day.
```

FIGURE 8–5   *Sample page from a security survey report.*

Again, note the logical division of the report into "Areas of Concern." How the work is divided is up to the individual consultant. One could easily regroup the areas of concern, in other ways, such as:

1. The Security Department
2. Physical Aspects of Security
3. Nonsecurity Operations
4. Policies and Procedures
5. Human Resources Management
6. Security Programs

Another characteristic of this alternative report is that, whereas in the standard report the findings and subsequent recommendations comprise distinctly separate sections of the report, the alternative approach immediately follows each finding with its related recommendation. *I tend to prefer this technique of offering the solutions to the problems as I go along, rather than to wait and offer them in group.*

Whatever report format the security consultant adopts, the presentation of the work must be professional: wordprocessed, error-free, clear, and pleasing to read. Make your report a work product your client would not hesitate to pass on to an executive in another firm. Bear in mind, too, that this document will be referred to over a span of years. Thus, it has the potential for use in a future civil lawsuit in which reasonable and adequate security may be the central issue... and you are accountable for your professional recommendations.

THE ORAL SURVEY

Occasionally, a client opts not to have the consultant prepare a written report of findings and recommendations, primarily to reduce consulting costs.

Additionally, a client may wish to hear what measures a professional would recommend but does not want to be bound by those recommendations. If the consultant, for example, recommends a uniformed security officer be on duty 24 hours a day as a deterrent to muggings in the parking lot, and management disagrees with that recommendation because of the expense of the guard, and a mugging does indeed subsequently occur, management would have a liability exposure. If a written security consultant's report exists, that document is *discoverable* in litigation. That written recommendation not followed tends to indict management. So management has become wary of being burdened with recommendations that could come home to haunt them.

Some consultants today offer, as a service option, an "oral survey." I do not, although I have been asked to conduct such surveys. Instead, a company representative accompanies me every step of the way through the survey and every moment on the site, and that person makes on-the-spot notes of my observations and recommendations. For example, I might observe that the seal number on a trailer being received from a distribution center is not being compared to or recorded on the transfer. I would advise the company representative to change the procedure to require that. The company representative would so note that observation and my suggestion for change. Later, in my absence, those notes would be transcribed into an internal report of my survey, and I may or may not be asked to review and correct them.

Chapter 9

Fees and Expenses

Fees and expenses have a critical impact upon the consulting profession. Realistically, one's survival as a consultant relates to one's fee structure. If you understate or undercharge for your services, the slim margin or actual absence of profit eventually will bring about a financial crisis. If, however, your fees are too high, prospective clients can afford limited—if any —of your services, and the ultimate result is, again, a financial crisis.

This means that your fees must be competitively balanced; they should fall within the range, albeit broad, of those acceptably charged within the security industry. In 1988 my informal survey of members of the International Association of Professional Security Consultants reflected a range of fees from $75.00 per hour to $175.00 per hour. I have attempted to keep track since then and now find, in the mid-1990s the low level is $100.00 and the high is $250.00. The variance in range obviously reflects such factors as expertise, experience, and reputation. In that connection, only a few weeks before writing this I was talking with a relatively new consultant who was charging $75.00 per hour and felt he was charging on the high side, if not overcharging! That is because he was comparing the hourly rate with private investigators. With all due respect to investigators, there is a substantial difference between the skills that are required between the two disciplines, plus, investigators are in abundance, whereas there are few consultants, in comparison. Certainly, nonmembers' fees probably range all over the board, particularly on the low side. This is because many so-called consultants have other sources of income, such as the sale of security-related hardware. This suggests a relationship between one's fees for services and the quality of those services: within general parameters, clients "get what they pay for."

As important as the hourly rate is (all consulting work must ultimately be broken down to an hourly unit of time), the fee should be based upon the actual *amount of time* required to do the consulting task. I have lost work bids to consultants and consulting firms who charge low and work slow. Perhaps the strategy of "charge low and work slow" is intentional, that is, it prolongs the project and hence increases the billing. Or perhaps it is a question of competency: Slow work seems thorough but could shield mediocrity.

The problem here is, how does the individual consultant win bids despite the tendency of many prospective clients to accept the lowest bidder? There is no one answer. This timeless irony is best expressed in the Latin: *caveat emptor*, let the buyer beware! Yet, we who charge higher fees have survived, apparently because we have confidence in our work, confidence in ourselves, and a reputation for quality in our work.

This in no way is meant to denigrate those who charge low fees. Some choose to maintain lower fees in order to be more sharply competitive. Others may opt to be busy at a lower rate than to have *dead time*.

For whatever reasons, the independent consultant will establish a fee that will thereafter set boundaries for all work. Whatever the hourly rate, a range of elements determines when and how to apply that rate. In the following, we will consider such items as:

field : office formula

travel time

advances

retainers

billing periods

expenses

the invoice

collection problems

FIELD : OFFICE FORMULA

New consultants often find themselves trapped in a situation where they have bid too low because they failed to include office time necessary to prepare the consultant's final report. Like the speaker who fails to include in the required fee the time it takes to prepare the speech, or the lecturer who fails to calculate the time necessary to design the presentation, the consultant must try to foresee all required time for a project before and after on-site work.

My formula simply applies a $1:\frac{1}{2}$ ratio; that is, for each one hour on a survey or with a client I calculate a half hour back in my office to sort through the notes, arrange my thoughts and findings in an intelligent order, and then prepare the finished report. As a sole practitioner, I prepare my own reports. That means I draft and compose as I proceed through my organized notes. One might say I am charging my client an exorbitant fee for clerical services—that the preparation of the report should be charged at a clerical rate. However, I end up saving the client the clerical costs because I must draft and compose anyway; this way I combine composition with wordprocessing.

Rare is the project that cannot be completed within the $1:\frac{1}{2}$ ratio. Rather, you usually can complete the project in less time than expected. That means your billing frequently comes to an amount less than the proposal, and the savings to the client, even if only an hour, is always appreciated.

Another bid option is to use the $1:\frac{1}{2}$ ratio in the estimation, along with a ceiling of a *not to exceed* or maximum cost for the client. Years ago, I quoted a project survey with report not to exceed $5,000. Exasperatingly, the operational vice president mysteriously disappeared in the midst of my field survey, and I was left stranded, unable to work. That unproductive time was reflected in my final billing as time spent on the project, and the total *actual cost* exceeded $5,000; yet the *amount due* showed as the not to exceed figure of $5,000. The actual invoice appeared as follows:

```
35.1 hours @ $150.00 per hour .....................................$5,265.00
     (12/13/XX, 12.1 hrs field survey)
     (12/14/XX, 9.4 hrs field survey)
     (12/15/XX, 6.7 hrs report preparation)
     (12/16/XX, 6.9 hrs report preparation)
Expenses: food & lodging ................  92.98
          220 mi @ 47 ¢  ................ 103.40
          report production  ..............  34.34
          Federal Express ................  20.25
                                  250.97 ...................      250.97
                                                              $5,515.97
Agreed NOT TO EXCEED cost ...................................$5,000.00
Less Advance .................................................$2,500.00
                                                              $2,500.00
                      TOTAL NOW DUE        $2,500.00
```

Every hour I committed to this client was duly reflected in the accounting of time and expenses. And because I promised to perform at a maximum figure, I billed only for that amount. That kind of underbilling may cost short-term profit for the consultant, but it also tends to build goodwill and credibility with your clientele.

TRAVEL TIME

The survey of IAPSC members reflected that most consultants bill their clients for travel time, although there were some variations, as follows:

1. One consultant charges only for one-way travel time; that is, if it takes two hours to get to the client's facility, he charges only two hours, not the full four hours for travel in both directions.
2. Another consultant charges for all time spent traveling, but at a different and lesser rate than is charged for consulting.
3. One consultant may or may not charge, depending on the distance, the client, and the workload involved.
4. As for me, I charge what is called "portal to portal," i.e., from the time I leave my office until I return to my office the meter is running and at my regular rate. If the trip is out-of-town and a stay in a hotel is required, I do not charge for the time I am in the hotel (unless I am working of course). I am charging for my time and the logic is the time traveling is time I could be otherwise productively engaged. I have made exceptions to this policy. That is the benefit of working for yourself, you can do what you want!

The majority of IAPSC members surveyed charged the client for all time beyond what the average person spends traveling to work each day.

ADVANCES

Most consultants require some form of advance or retainer for work to be done. An *advance* is a partial payment for services to be rendered. It represents good faith on the part of the purchasing client. Recently I finalized an agreement over the telephone and, during that conversation, I requested one-half of the agreed-upon fee in advance. The executive said he would be happy to have the check cut and forwarded immediately. When I complete this project and send him the bound report, the final invoice will reflect total fees plus expenses, less the advance. Had this executive been unable to forward the advance, I might tend to get nervous about his firm's ability to pay.

To obtain an advance against work to be performed certainly is optional but in some cases might be financially prudent, depending on the stability of the client, the total cost of the consulting project, the anticipated length of the project, and anticipated expenses for the project. However, one may not wish to require or even request an advance from an established former client.

Advances may range anywhere from 25 to 50 percent of the expected total; or, the advance may reflect expenses only, (airfare, food, and lodging) to avoid out-of-pocket expenditures to the consultant.

RETAINERS

Retainers may also serve as an advance against billing but also may refer to an ongoing relationship with a given client. For a retainer fee, the consultant is available for an agreed-upon amount of time each month. This typically takes the form of monthly payments of a specified amount to guarantee that the consultant will be available for specified hours or days each month. The client might, for example, guarantee one day's fee to cover the monthly needs of the client. The retainer may represent the consultant's normal billing rate or, because it is an ongoing relationship and the consultant may or may not work on that day, the retainer fee may be at a discounted rate, even as low as 50 percent of the normal rate. Hence, the consultant with a $200 rate may be on a retainer for one day a month at half-rate, $100 per hour, which equals $800 a month. If she or he does not work, the $800 rate is still collected for the consultant standing by. If work is required that month, the first eight hours are billed at the lower rate and all subsequent hours would be billed at the regular rate.

The consultant in some cases may allow the client to accumulate unused time for up to one year (normally at the full rate), and at the end of the year the slate is wiped clean and the new year starts anew. Obviously, there is room for a great deal of flexibility and creativity in retainer arrangements.

Consultants have mixed feelings regarding retainerships. Some people are simply more comfortable with a dependable commitment and guaranteed (even if discounted) income than in facing the unknown. Yet, this may contradict the character of the individual who opts for the independence of a consulting career vis-à-vis the security of a corporate position.

BILLING PERIODS

Typically, the consultant bills the client at the conclusion of the consulting assignment. If the assignment spans more than one calendar month, you may bill monthly for "services and expenses to date."

EXPENSES

Expenses incurred by the consultant that may be billed to the client include:

1. Travel costs
   a. use of the consultant's private auto
   b. public transportation (planes, trains, taxis)
   c. lodging
   d. meals
   e. gratuities
2. Clerical services, telephone and telegraphic costs, parcel/package delivery, and printing/binding costs
3. Miscellaneous expenses
   a. researcher costs
   b. outside investigative costs
   c. photographic costs

Excepting individual client limitations on reimbursable expenses, and legal limitations imposed by the Internal Revenue Service, you may set your own standards. For example, I bill clients 49¢ a mile for the use of my private auto. Some clients may limit auto mileage reimbursement to 25¢ per mile as a matter of policy. If indeed such a client objected to my rate, I would acquiesce to their corporate guidelines. The same is true with air transportation. I fly first class only; so do a few of the IAPSC members surveyed. I might pay the difference between coach and first class if, for example, the CEO of the client company always flies coach as a matter of policy.

Unless the client specifically asks for you to submit copies of receipts, do not attach them to the invoice. Although proof of expenses need not accompany the invoice, such receipts should be retained as part of the file as a sound business practice as well as evidence in the event of an IRS audit.

Some consultants pass on to the client *actual only* expenses, while others add on a *service charge* of about 5 percent. Either way is proper. Of course, a 5 percent service charge would not be added if the client had made an advance against expenses.

Now these expenses you bill your client for end up appearing as income, e.g., you bill the client $5,000.00 for your services plus $1,000.00 for such expenses as airfare, hotel, taxis, etc. The client sends a check for $6,000.00 which you record as income. In a very real way the expenses you bill for "inflate" your income and at the end of the year you must deduct such expenses from the gross receipts or you will pay income tax on the reimbursement of your own expenses. Put another way, you have two sources of income: revenue from services provided *and* the legitimate deduction of expenses, because every dollar you do not deduct as a legitimate expense you *pay* tax on!

THE INVOICE

The invoice is the document that presents your billing to the client. It serves as a demand for payment for services rendered and expenses incurred. This instrument is carefully reviewed by the client, who notes such components as the amount of time spent. If the invoice is reasonable and meets expectations, it is approved and forwarded for payment.

The invoice may appear on the consultant's letterhead, a preprinted business form, or a computerized statement (see Figures 9–1 through 9–5). Note how Figures 9–1, 9–4 and 9–5 break the time into tenths of an hour whereas the other two invoices reflect even hours. Personally, I believe the more specific the billing the better.

I encourage the numbering of invoices because that way, an invoice log can list how many invoices you have prepared this year to date, to whom, on what date, and for what amount—and which ones are still outstanding. See Figure 9–6 for an example of an invoice log.

Some consultants require the invoice be paid within a specified period of time (usually 30 days) and add a penalty of 1% to $1\frac{1}{2}$% of the invoice total if not paid within that time. Should you use this strategy, you must be certain that it is clearly spelled out on the invoice itself.

Invoices should be prepared in duplicate with one copy retained for your file. In rare cases an invoice gets lost, and upon request you can pull the duplicate and send a photocopy for processing. The duplicate also memorializes, for the file, your time and expenses on that client's project. I also recommend that your IRS number (or social security number) be displayed on the invoice, in view of the IRS requirement that such payments be reported. Unless your client already has your number, its absence could cause delays in the payment. Some firms will not pay until they have the number. Others may make payment and request the number at the close of the year. Placing the number on each statement simply expedites the process.

CRIME AND LOSS REDUCTION   (619) 749-7527

CHARLES A. SENNEWALD & ASSOCIATES
SECURITY MANAGEMENT CONSULTING

June 15, 1995

John D. Sonderson, Esq.
JUDD, SONDERSON, MYERS, WILLITS & TYLER
Suite 1800
2888 Bryan Blvd.
Dallas, Texas 75201

Re: Backer v. Midwest Freehold, et al.

Dear Mr. Sonderson:

Following is my closing invoice re the above captioned matter:

30.6 hours @ $250.00 per hour.................................$7,650.00

    [6/4/95, .6 hr. file set-up, correspond]
    [6/7/95, 5.3 hrs. review 1-3, part of 4, telecon]
    [6/8/95, 5.1 hrs. complete 4, review 5 & 6]
    [6/9/95, .3 hr. review 7, telecon]
    [6/12/95, 5.7 hrs. log-in new materials, travel]
    [6/13/95, 12.2 hrs. meeting/site inspection/travel]
    [6/14/95, 1.1 hrs. draft prelim opinion, fax, telecon]
    [6/15/95, .3 hr. close file, invoice]

Expenses: Long distance calls................   36.15
          Airfare........................... 1,036.00
          Dallas taxi.......................   34.00
          80 mi. in San Diego @ 49¢ per......   39.20
          San Diego parking.................   30.00
          Food/lodging......................   174.14
          Tips..............................   6.00
                        1,355.49..... 1,355.49
                                          $9,005.49

                            Less Retainer........... 1,250.00
                                          7,755.49

Invoice #1618   TOTAL NOW DUE........... $7,755.49
Tax I.D. #559-38-4142

Thank you.

Charles A. Sennewald, CMC, CPP
CAS:cs

      28004 LAKE MEADOW DRIVE, ESCONDIDO, CALIFORNIA 92026

FIGURE 9–1   *Invoice for forensic work.*

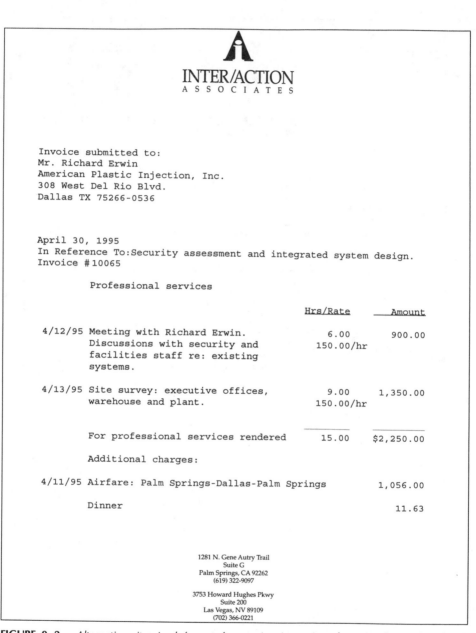

FIGURE 9–2 *Alternative, itemized format for an invoice using the consultant's letterhead.
(Reproduced by permission of Steve Kaufer, CPP.)*

A

Mr. Richard Erwin   Page   2

		Amount
4/12/95	Lunch	9.75
	Dinner	10.39
4/13/95	Lodging	346.32
	Lunch	7.95
	Dinner	18.25
	Car rental	89.85
	Total costs	$1,550.14
	Total amount of this bill	$3,800.14
	Balance due	$3,800.14

NET 15 DAYS
THANK YOU

Please make payments to:
Inter/Action Associates, Inc.
3753 Howard Hughes Parkway
Las Vegas, NV 89109
ID# 88-4254432

FIGURE 9–2   *Continued.*

COLLECTION PROBLEMS

Collection problems are rare. Problems that do arise include:

The client **refuses to pay any amount.**
The client **refuses to pay part of the amount.**
The client **delays payment.**

```
                           STATEMENT
                 STRATEGIC CONTROLS, INC.
                        244 MADISON AVENUE
                     NEW YORK, NEW YORK 10016
                          212-724-7400


                                     DATE  9-8-94

     ┌                                              ┐
   •   Whidby Industries Corp.
       356 Mustang Dr.
       Boston, MA   02180

       Attn:  D.W. Chase, Ex. V.P.

     └                                              ┘
       DETACH AND MAIL WITH YOUR CHECK.    YOUR CANCELLED CHECK IS YOUR RECEIPT.


                           I N V O I C E

   9-1-94      For Professional Services
               Security Audit & Survey
               Distribution Center
               715 Cascade Ave.
               Lynn, MA   02150

               9-1,2 & 3:
               Audit & Survey  -  22 hours

               9-4 & 5:
               Report Writing  -  10  hours

               32 hours @ $150. per hour        $ 4,800.00

               Expenses:
                   76 miles @ $0.30 per mile         22.80
                   Tolls                              9.00
                   Phone                              6.10
                   Photo processing                  12.35
                   Extra copies                       5.60
                                                   ──────────
                                     TOTAL       $ 4,855.85

               IRS #   73-17843
```

FIGURE 9–3   *Preprinted invoice form.*

Refusal to Pay Any Amount

I know of one case wherein a major security service firm contracted a security audit, and the consultant's survey report was of such poor quality that the client rejected the report and refused to pay. The security firm then asked if I would

THOMAS D. ROEMER, CPP
Security Consulting & Design
1540 Bunescu Court
Buffalo Grove, Illinois 60089
Tel. & Fax 708-913-0666

DATE: March 1, 1995	**INVOICE NO.** 1281
CLIENT: WORLDWIDE SECURITY GROUP 120 Forest Dr. Suite 380 The Woodlands, TX. 77380	**PROJECT:** CHEMICO Monterrey, Mex.
ATTN: Mr. Phil Thompson	**TERMS:** Net 30 days

DESCRIPTION OF SERVICES	AMOUNT
This invoice is for security consulting services and expenses incurred during the month of February 1995, and consists of the following: **Consulting Time** Thomas D. Roemer - 56.5 hours @ $85.00/hr	$4,802.50
Subtotal Time	**$4,802.50**
Reimbursable Expenses Hotel in Monterrey Taxi & Limo Travel + Tip Long Distance Phone Airfare Meals + Tips	$ 343.68 126.90 86.90 385.35 50.00
Subtotal Expenses	$ 992.83
TOTAL	$5,795.33

Signed: *Thomas D. Roemer, CPP*

1815TGG.INV

FIGURE 9–4   *Computerized statement generated from a personal computer.*

conduct the survey for that same client. Thus, the security firm suffered a loss in the cost of their own survey but provided another security professional to do the project for the disgruntled client.

If a client refused to pay but the consultant felt confident that the contract had been met, the only recourse available would be to collect through the courts.

JRS Security Services, Inc.

3179 Danmark Drive • West Friendship, Md. 21794 • 410 • 442 • 1756

March 20, 1995

Mr. Jerry Chambers
American Personal Communications
One Democracy Center
6901 Rockledge Drive
Suite 600
Bethesda, Md. 20817

Dear Jerry,

My invoice for services rendered, pursuant to our agreement, for consulting services for the period of March 3 through March 18, 1995 follows:

INVOICE

Meetings and coordination for security system, and security officer review at 6901 Rockledge Drive; Review plans for new projected space at Democracy Center; Conduct Security Survey for Warehouse facility at Beltsville, Md.; Prepare Key Control guidelines; Prepare survey reports for Beltsville warehouse and APC Bethesda Headquarters

28.5 Hours @ $ 150.00 .... $ 4,275.00
                                                    ===========

                                            TOTAL $ 4,275.00

Thank you for allowing me to assist you with your security program.

Sincerely,

John R. Smith

John R. Smith, CPP

Fed Tax #: 52-1705002

FIGURE 9–5　*An invoice without itemized expenses because (1) the assignment is local and (2) minor expenses are absorbed as a cost of doing business.*

Refusal to Pay a Part of the Amount

I know of another case in which the client objected to the amount of *time* billed, because there was no explanation as to what work was performed during that

INVOICE LOG				
#	Date	Client	Amount	Date Paid
95001	1-11-95	GALLAGHER & ASSOC.	4,216.86	2-16-95
95002	1-17-95	PELL MANUFACTURING	1,986.21	2-1-95
95003	1-24-95	MONTVALE, STONE & KLEIN	406.55	
95004	1-27-95	STONE INDUSTRIES	909.37	3-10-95
95005	2-9-95	BROWN, BROWN & HILL	2,776.50	
95006				
95007				

FIGURE 9–6   *Invoice log.*

period of time. To avoid such a problem, the consultant can itemize tasks for the various hours billed.

Delayed Payment

This represents the most common and irksome problem that faces consultants. Most companies pay invoices within a thirty-day period. If the invoice is not paid promptly and thirty days after the date of billing the invoice remains outstanding, you may send a copy of the original invoice with SECOND NOTICE stamped in red ink. You will likely be paid promptly. Personally, I prefer a telephone call to that executive with whom I worked, and that tends to resolve the problem.

A final solution to any uncollectable bill may be to enforce payment through the courts. If the amount is not too large, small claims court may provide the most effective forum. Documentation, which the consultant should always keep, carries a great deal of persuasive weight in these courts. And using a small claims court helps you bypass attorneys' or a collection agency's fees. If the amount due exceeds the limits of the small claims court, then the most appropriate course of action could entail retaining an attorney for the filing of a lawsuit. The courts should be a last resort, after polite telephone calls and letters fail.

Chapter 10

Forensic Consulting

The word *Forensic* is defined in the American Heritage Dictionary as "pertaining to or employed in legal proceedings or argumentation." Forensic consulting, therefore, involves the consultant's services in cases of litigation. Whereas management consulting entails a *proactive* (beforehand) assessment of security needs in which the consultant reports to managers of an enterprise, forensic consulting is the *reactive* (after the fact) assessment of security issues as a service to a law firm representing either management (the defendant) or the complainant (the plaintiff).

Security forensic consultants assist litigations that address the issue of alleged security negligence.

THE NEED FOR SECURITY CONSULTANTS IN LEGAL CASES

Lawsuits that evolve around security issues fall into two categories:

1. *Third party crimes*: For example, a visitor (first party) comes to a local hospital (second party) and while walking back to her automobile in the hospital's parking lot is abducted and sexually assaulted by a stranger (third party). The question in this kind of lawsuit is: Was the security program adequate or inadequate? Was the hospital careless or negligent in its duty to make parking in the lot reasonably safe for visitors? Was the hospital on notice that the lot was not safe because of a number of crimes there? Did the hospital have a duty to make the lot safe because of such notice?

The component parts of this kind of civil litigation are:

Notice of a problem
A duty
A breach of that duty
The breach was the proximate cause of the injury
As a result of the injury the person was damaged

The foreseeability of an event is what establishes a duty. And foreseeability or predictability is based on historical experience as well as what a reasonable

AGREEMENT

DAVID L. BERGER
SECURITY CONSULTANT

11600 Montana Avenue / Los Angeles, CA 90049 / (310) 826-7386

1.   This agreement is between DAVID L. BERGER, hereinafter referred to as "CONSULTANT" and the undersigned, hereinafter referred to as the "CONSULTEE".

2.   Consultant agrees to furnish Consultee with his best efforts in studying all pertinent research materials and documentation, provided by the Consultee, relating to the matter for which he was retained along with any physical inspections or site surveys necessary toward formulating an opinion relative to the issue at hand.

3.   The Consultant further agrees to make himself available to testify at any deposition, hearing or trial where this issue is the subject of that proceeding.

4.   The Consultee agrees to pay the Consultant the sum of One Hundred Eighty-Five Dollars ($185.00) per hour for all time expended on behalf of the Consultee, plus travel time and expenses necessary for work performed away from the Consultant's premises.

5.   The Consultee agrees to pay the Consultant a non-refundable minimum fee retainer of Nine Hundred Dollars ($900.00) and to meet all other requirements contained in the Consultant's "FEE SCHEDULE" which is attached to, and forms a portion of, this agreement.

6.   Consultee agrees that any deposition required will be at a rate of One Hundred Eighty-Five Dollars ($185.00) per hour with a minimum fee required of Seven Hundred Forty Dollars ($740.00), according to the attached "FEE SCHEDULE" and that proper notification and arrangements will be made on the Consultant's behalf with the deposing attorney. Payment should be rendered at the time of the deposition. Should the minimum fee exceed that approved by the Court as the deposing attorney's obligation, the Consultee will be charged the remaining balance.

7.   Consultee agrees that the Consultant, in order to retain his objectivity and professional decorum in the eyes of the courts, cannot and will not accept gratuities or bonuses should the matter be successfully adjudicated; nor would it be appropriate to accept an assignment on a contingency basis. It is important that the Consultant's conclusions and opinions not be influenced by extra financial considerations.

(Continued on other side)

FIGURE 10–1   *Example of a forensic consultant's agreement. (Reproduced by permission of David L. Berger.)*

person could expect in a given set of circumstances, i.e., even if a new hospital is being constructed (hence, no on-site history of crime) we can reasonably predict that unless a certain level of security is provided in the parking lots at that facility, such as lighting, security patrols and/or CCTV monitoring, etc., someone will be assaulted.

2

8. Consultee agrees that he/she will be personally responsible and liable for payment of all charges billed by the Consultant, irrespective of whether services are performed for or on behalf of a client or clients of Consultee, and that all monies due will be paid immediately upon presentation of Consultant's statement of charges. Payment will not be predicated upon, nor will it await, final settlement or adjudication of the matter.

Further, Consultee agrees to pay interest on all balances remaining unpaid after thirty days from presentation of Consultant's statement at a rate of twelve percent (12%) per annum; however, in no event will interest be charged at a rate higher than allowed by applicable law. In such cases where the above rate exceeds the highest rate allowed by applicable law then, in that event, Consultee agrees to be charged interest on such balances at the highest rate permitted by such law.

9. Consultee agrees to pay any attorney's fees, court and other costs necessary for the Consultant to seek legal assistance in collecting fees.

10. Consultee agrees to indemnify and hold harmless the Consultant from any claims or actions arising from the Consultant's employment on the Consultee's behalf.

11. After careful study, analysis and consideration of all the materials presented to the Consultant by the Consultee, along with any other related studies or investigations, the Consultant agrees to present his findings in an honest, unbiased and forthright manner both to the Consultee and at deposition, trial or other hearings.

It should be noted that many times the Consultant's findings and ultimate professional opinion are not entirely consistent with the Consultee's client's position in the law suit. The Consultant believes it would be a disservice to the Consultee NOT to advise him of the actual circumstances relative to the issue. This is, after all, an effort to assist the Consultee in the manner by which he will represent his client and to guide him relative to the position of the opposition who, in many instances, are also being advised by a competent consultant.

CONSULTANT: CONSULTEE:

DAVID L. BERGER
                                      _____
                                      FIRM NAME

_____   By:_____
Signature   (Authorized Signature)

_____   _____
DATE   DATE

FIGURE 10-1   *Continued.*

2. *Torts involving alleged negligence as committed (or omitted) by the defendant:* For example, a retail security agent arrests a person for shoplifting when in fact no theft was committed. The customer is subsequently released in exchange for a written admission of guilt. Depending upon state law, the conduct of the agent may be challenged. Such questions arise as: Was the stopping of the customer proper and was the obtaining of a written admission extortionate? Was the agent adequately trained? Were the arrest procedures and policies of the agent's employer in keeping with the law as well as custom and practice in the industry?

Questions of civil liability and negligence are concerns of the legal profession. Although most security consultants are not attorneys, they must confront issues and problems such as these when dealing in the forensic field. The security consultant simply makes an assessment of all the known facts surrounding the incident in question and forms an opinion as to the adequacy or inadequacy of security, or the proper or improper conduct of the security employee. Legal professionals seek advice from the security expert.

True experts know their limitations. As an example, I was contacted by a San Francisco law firm who asked if I could review the security program of a local airline. The program was breached by a disgruntled former airline employee who shot the pilot and copilot of an inflight airliner, causing the crash of the plane and the death of all aboard. Although security principles generally apply from industry to industry, this case was beyond my expertise, so I referred the law firm to another consultant who I knew had credentials specific to this case.

Consultants who accept forensic work should not approach the assignment as an advocate. Advocacy is the role for the attorney, not for the professional consultant whose role is *objectively* to review the facts and express an opinion regarding the meritoriousness of the case, no matter who retained her or his services.

Regrettably, some consultants and so-called expert witnesses have earned the reputation of being *guns-for-hire*: the legal profession refers to them as whores. These consultants will make a case to support the position represented by the law firm that retained them. Some law firms *do* want an expert to act as an advocate while the majority want an objective opinion for guidance in their own assessment of the case. I will not assist a firm that seeks an advocate expert.

Granted, the security consultant who is retained by a plaintiff law firm to critique the program of a professional security department risks, in some cases, the ire of the security chief. On the other hand, I have heard of security department directors who have privately agreed with the basis of a lawsuit, saying they knew the security program was inadequate, that they had requested the resources to correct it, but senior management ignored their advice and recommendations.

Ironically, the security industry can benefit when a significant award goes against a corporation in this type of situation. A large settlement often has awakened the need for a reassessment of the security and loss-prevention role in the corporate organization. Security negligence, as in the example of the hospital lawsuit, raises additional questions for the legal profession:

1. Did the hospital have a duty of care, a duty to protect the visitor from strangers attacking her?
2. Was the attack foreseeable?
3. Was management of the hospital aware of the risks to visitors in the parking lot? If not, should officials have been aware?
4. What reasonable steps did management actually take to reduce the possibility of attacks occurring in the parking lot?

So, the security consultant reviewing the facts in connection with this hospital case would be asked for an opinion about these questions.

THE PROCESS OF FORENSIC CONSULTING

Forensic consulting follows a rather prescribed process that typically unfolds as follows:

The consultant is queried about availability.

The consultant either declines or agrees to proceed.

The consultant reviews the materials.

The consultant reaches an opinion.

The consultant is deposed.

The consultant testifies in trial.

Let us review each of these to gain insight into what each step entails.

The Consultant Is Queried about Availability

The most common query comes by telephone. An attorney will call and identify the firm as representing one side or another in a lawsuit. If the consultant specializes in forensic work, the attorney may identify the case style or caption, for example, John Doe v. National Oil, to determine if there is any conflict of interest. Examples of conflict might be: you have already been retained by the opposite side, you serve or have served as a consultant to National Oil, your brother is John Doe, or for any other reason you cannot or would not involve yourself in that lawsuit.

The attorney then asks if you have expertise and interest in gasoline company service stations, because the case at hand involves the robbery and shooting to death of an employee of a National Oil Company leased station. The attorney represents the deceased's surviving wife and family. If you feel qualified for this kind of security case and agree to have the attorney give a brief scenario, the attorney proceeds.

The theory of liability in this suit is that National Oil mandates that all leased stations must be open twenty-four hours a day, even those stations in the inner city, areas considered dangerous during night and early morning hours. Yet National Oil failed to provide promised security equipment such as cameras, bullet-resistant glass, and pass-through cashier drawers. Meanwhile, the employee was shot and killed by robbers at 3:00 A.M. The attorney sees National Oil's failure to provide the equipment as negligence and sees such negligence as the proximate cause of the crime (directly related to the cause of the robbery and shooting).

Irrespective of the kind of plaintiff case the attorney has, more often than not I ask what his theory of liability is (examples: security officer was inadequately trained, used excessive force, falsified documents, was not really on the job but was across the street in a bar drinking beer, etc.). Some theories of liability appear to be appropriate in relationship to the factual scenario, others may lack merit or are even ridiculous.

If the attorney represents the defendant I usually ask what the theory of defense is, as he sees it (examples: the attack in the parking lot was an unforeseeable event, the plaintiff was careless and placed herself in the way of harm, or the alleged security failure was not the proximate cause of the attack and injury). Some theories, again, appear reasonable and others lack merit, depending of course on the brief factual scenario as described by the lawyer. And remember, the lawyer is obviously an advocate for his case.

The consultant must recognize that the so-called "factual scenario" does not represent all the facts of the lawsuit and no opinions can possibly be formed at this juncture, but it should provide enough insight into the matter to enable the consultant to decline involvement or agree to review the facts.

Those just entering this field of forensic consulting should be aware of a growing belief and/or practice on the part of some attorneys of deliberately calling qualified consultants, discussing the case under the ruse of seriously considering them for retention, only to attempt to disqualify or "neutralize" each one of them on the basis that he had discussed the case with them and therefore it would be improper for the consultant to accept the assignment for the opposing side. I personally view this practice as unethical. The very thought that an officer of the court (an attorney admitted to the bar) would intentionally contaminate available experts so his opponent would be denied such resources as well as create a condition that effectively denies consultants their livelihood is wrong. Do not be trapped or inhibited by this practice.

On the other hand, the practice of an attorney actually retaining more than one consultant, especially those who are deemed top-drawer experts, is viewed as an acceptable (but expensive) practice.

The Consultant Either Declines or Agrees to Proceed

Now is decision time. The consultant either declines involvement or indicates he has an interest in assisting. Declination is usually because of actual or perceived conflict of interests, lack of the required expertise, a gut instinct that the matter lacks merit (in his own private and professional view, albeit he has only a brief scenario to go on), perhaps does not like the sound of the attorney, or the time constraints preclude his involvement. It is not uncommon for law firms to delay incurring the cost of experts until late in the game and then there is a scramble to find a qualified expert who has time to immediately undertake the task. Fortunately not all lawyers are so disposed.

If the consultant expresses an interest in the case, i.e., makes himself a viable candidate for selection as the attorney's consultant, there invariably is a discussion about fees and the attorney's interest in obtaining a copy of the consultant's curriculum vitae, commonly referred to as a C.V., which is like a resume. (see Figure 10–2). The statement of fees (fee schedule) and C.V. is usually faxed to the attorney's office at that time.

CHARLES A. SENNEWALD, CMC, CPP
Curriculum Vitae

EMPLOYMENT HISTORY
- Air Policeman, USAF, 3½ years
- Deputy Sheriff, Los Angeles County, 6 years
- Chief of Security, Claremont Colleges, 2 years
- Director of Security, The Broadway Department Stores
  (52 major stores in 4 states), 18 years

TEACHING HISTORY
- Lecturer, Chaffey and Orange Coast Colleges, 1 year
- Assistant Professor, California State University at Los Angeles, 13 years

EDUCATION
- BS Degree, Police Science & Administration, California State University at Los Angeles

LITERARY CONTRIBUTIONS
- Author of four college and trade textbooks:
  - *Effective Security Management,* Sec. World Pub., 1978, 2nd Ed., 1985
  - *The Process of Investigation,* Butterworth Pub., 1981
  - *Security Consulting,* Butterworth Pub., 1989, 2nd Ed., 1995
  - *Shoplifting,* (co-authored) Butterworth-Heinemann Pub., 1992
- Author of numerous articles published in trade journals and the *Protection of Assets Manuals,* Merritt Co. Pub.

PROFESSIONAL AFFILIATIONS AND ACCOMPLISHMENTS
- Founder and first President, International Association of Professional Security Consultants
- Holder of the professional designation Certified Management Consultant, CMC
- Holder of the professional designation Certified Protection Professional, CPP
- Member, American Society for Industrial Security
- Member, Institute of Management Consultants
- Past president and member, International Foundation for Protection Officers (Canada)
- 1979 recipient of Security World Magazine's Merit Award
- U.S. Security Industry Representative to Stockholm and Copenhagen in 1981 and to Hong Kong, Taipei and Tokyo in 1983, by appointment of the U.S. Department of Commerce
- 1995 recipient of the IAPSC's Distinguished Service Accolade

CURRENTLY (1979 TO THE PRESENT)
- Consultant to corporate management
- Consultant to the legal profession
- Security industry seminar lecturer

CHARLES A. SENNEWALD, CMC, CPP • 28004 Lake Meadow Drive • Escondido, CA 92026 • (619) 749-7527

FIGURE 10-2 *Sample C.V.*

The decision to proceed now rests with the attorney, to retain or not to retain. That decision is usually based on such factors as the consultant's reputation, his fees, location of the court in relation to where the consultant resides, and probably, to some degree, what impression the consultant makes on the attorney during the phone conversation.

Most consultants require a retainer fee along with a letter confirming the retention. Most have a non-refundable retainer representing either a flat fee or, as in my case, five hours of work.

Now surfaces a particularly thorny problem over which we consultants have very little control, and that is the issue of a given consultant being declared as an expert witness by an attorney with whom you have discussed a case by phone and indicated your willingness to assist yet have not been retained! Put another way, the attorney claims in documents submitted to the court you are his expert, he uses your C.V. to spell out your qualifications to serve as his expert, and states, in that declaration you will be willing to testify to a variety of opinions and he even articulates specific opinions and you are not even aware this has occurred. No matter how you slice it, this is a misrepresentation made to the court and to the opposing counsel. And this is becoming a frequent practice. To add injury to insult, the consultant is not even compensated for the use of his "intellectual property" when it clearly is a designed strategy to flex the muscles of the attorney's case, as well as enhance the possibility of a settlement, without incurring the expense of retaining an expert.

This is not to suggest that the majority of law firms engage in this practice. Clearly they do not. But those of us who are active in forensic consulting see it growing at an alarming rate. One consultant (not in the security discipline) established he had been declared as an expert without his knowledge or permission, and without compensation, over 1,000 times and filed a lawsuit against a number of firms for that practice.

In an effort to combat this, some enlightened consultants have adopted the practice of sending a follow-up letter to each attorney with whom they have talked and sent a C.V. to, stating, in essence, that 30 days have passed since their discussion and that as the consultant has not heard from the attorney, the consultant assumes that the attorney has elected to retain another consultant or has resolved the matter. Therefore, it is understood that there is no business relationship and the consultant is free to accept inquiries by and/or engagements with any other parties regarding this matter. It is amazing how many retainer checks that letter generates!

Another strategy followed by consultants is, upon learning they have been declared as an expert, simply to invoice for the retainer amount.

I personally made a complaint to the California State Bar about this practice and the matter is unresolved at the time of this writing. Surely this is an issue the legal profession across the country will address in due time. Until then, be alert to the problem.

The Consultant Reviews the Materials

Any time from a matter of days to one year later, depending upon the urgency of the matter, materials from the attorney along with the retainer are received. The materials usually include a cover letter listing what has been transmitted for the review, along with the agreed-upon retainer.

The materials I typically request include:

- the police report of the incident in question
- the plaintiff's complaint
- interrogatories and responses of both parties
- requests for production of documents from both sides, and the responses received
- the depositions that pertain to the issue of liability (as opposed to damages)
- any criminal court proceedings and testimony, if appropriate and available

I recommend numbering each document and logging the documents on the front page of a tablet in which the notes of the review will be recorded (see Figure 10–3). I then paginate the tablet, so that the table of contents of the documents reviewed allows for ease in referencing a given document.

The review requires the extraction of salient information, key points that can be reviewed as a refresher prior to a meeting with attorneys or the presentation of testimony in court (see Figure 10–4). Invariably, as the review progresses, certain questions will be raised, or further discovery or research required, and these needs may be noted in the margin, as reflected in Figure 10–4.

The Consultant Reaches an Opinion

The review is the process whereby the expert can formulate an opinion as to the conditions of the case. If the expert has been retained by the law firm representing the plaintiff, the task is to determine, *in the consultant's opinion*, whether the case is meritorious. The expert is sought for the purpose of rendering an opinion, and if it favors the attorney's position, then that opinion is offered in the form of an affidavit and/or sworn testimony.

It should be noted that only recognized "experts" are allowed to express opinions in our judicial system. All other witnesses are restricted to factual testimony. If the expert's opinion is unfavorable, however, chances are rare indeed that she or he ever will testify.

The consultant may not need to review all the material provided to reach an opinion. I recall one case in which I had been retained to review a plaintiff action against a retailer for false arrest and imprisonment. I had assisted the same firm in a similar case some years earlier and the plaintiff had prevailed. Midway through this new assignment I called the attorney and advised him of the materials I had reviewed and what remained, and asked if he could direct me to a specific document in the yet-unread materials that might throw a different light on the case, because I found no fault in the retailer's conduct. I also advised him there was no point in my continuing with the review and incurring expenses if there were no new facts that addressed the issue of probable cause for the arrest. That concluded my work! As disappointed as he was, he now had an authoritative analysis of his case that suggested it lacked merit.

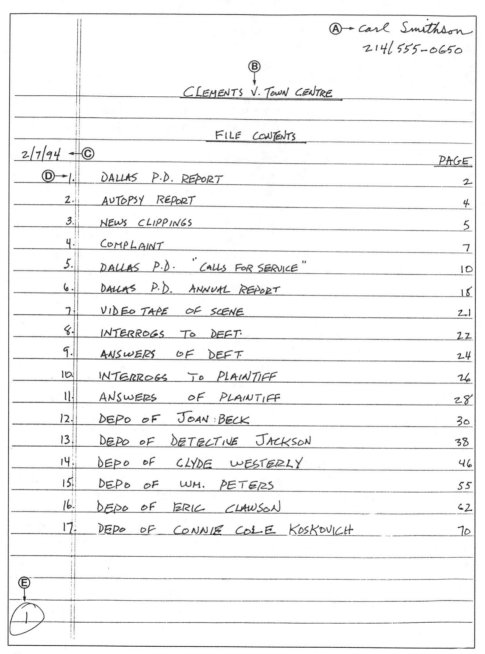

FIGURE 10-3 *Notepad table of contents listing review notes taken on each document. (A) Attorney's name and phone number, (B) "Style" or caption of lawsuit, (C) Date of incident, (D) Materials reviewed, and (E) Page number.*

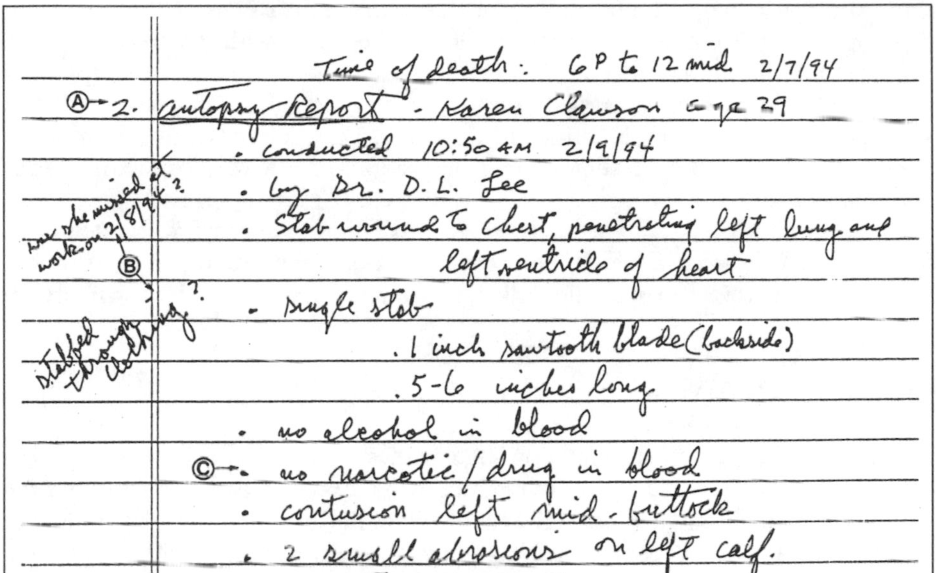
Time of death: 6P to 12 mid 2/7/94

Ⓐ→ 2. Autopsy Report - Karen Clawson age 29
- conducted 10:50 AM 2/9/94
- by Dr. D. L. Lee
- Stab wound to chest, penetrating left lung and left ventricle of heart
- single stab
  - 1 inch sawtooth blade (backside)
  - 5-6 inches long
- no alcohol in blood
- Ⓒ→ no narcotic/drug in blood
- contusion left mid-buttock
- 2 small abrasions on left calf.
- direction of wound:
  - front to back
  - from above, downward, and
  - slightly from left to right
- jewelry present: mexican coin ring
  yellow metal watch
  yellow metal ring w/red stone

was she missed at work on 2/8/94?

Ⓑ

stabbed through clothing?

valued jewelry?

Ⓓ

4

FIGURE 10–4 *Sample page of review notes, with questions in the margin. (A) Document reviewed, (B) Questions that need answers, (C) Notes on document, (D) Page number.*

My experience is that the consultant reaches an opinion at some point in time prior to the completion of the assessment in its totality, and all work performed beyond that point tends to enhance or buttress the opinion.

You form this opinion through site inspection—a visit to and inspection of the premises—if the nature of the litigation warrants this. To view the configuration of a parking lot; its relationship to the facility it serves; and the types of lighting, landscaping, perimeter, and access devices; brings into focus the scene of the problem.

Once you reach an opinion (assuming for this example the case is meritorious), that position usually is conveyed during a phone conversation with the attorney.

The fact that an expert has been retained must be disclosed to the opposing side and that opposition is entitled to know such expert's position prior to trial. In some states the opposition is entitled to the expert's opinion in writing, prior to the consultant's taking of his testimony in a deposition. In other states the opinion is surfaced in the deposition only.

A word is necessary about the need to resist those attorneys who attempt to formulate or otherwise influence the consultant's opinion. Certainly most attorneys are not guilty of this form of manipulation, but some are. Beware of the possibility.

The Consultant Is Deposed

A *deposition* is the oral examination of a witness, under oath, by the opposing attorney(s). The objective of an examination of an expert witness is to explore the expert's credentials and discover the expert's opinions, prior to trial. The testimony is recorded by a court reporter and, although the setting seems somewhat casual, the results bear the same weight as though the proceedings were in an actual court of law.

There is an increasing use of video-taped depositions to supplement the official typed transcript of the testimony. Subsequent viewing of the videotape allows the opposition to critique the witness' appearance and communication skills as well as to determine how the witness will come across in trial.

Although the objective of the deposition is to examine the witness, the occasion affords the witness an opportunity to assess the competency and personality of the examining attorney. Some attorneys approach the process with a professional and objective air and proceed smoothly in discovering the information they need to do their job. Others may act unpleasant, officious, or inept.

You run the risk of being examined by an attorney who views you as an adversary. Some take advantage of the deposition to intimidate witnesses, hence stretching the bounds of propriety outside the view of the judge and jury. Such counselors tend to be more judicious in the presence of a jury for fear of alienating them. Jurors demand fair play.

Whatever the style, tack, or method of the attorney's interrogation, the expert witness should rise to the level of professionalism but never stoop to anything less. Be pleasant and courteous at all times and under all circumstances. Be succinct but complete in your answers. Needless to say, be impeccably honest and truthful in every answer.

Do not volunteer information. Just answer each question; nothing more or less.

Whatever notes or files you bring into the deposition, the examining attorney is entitled to examine and make copies of them. I welcome that scrutiny, because it tends to reflect the thoroughness and quality of my work.

The opposing law firm usually is obliged to pay for your time and expenses in connection with the deposition. Require your fee and expenses prior to testifying, to avoid a possible collection problem later.

Subsequent to your deposition, you will receive the transcript for your review, correction, and signature. If your answers require any change or correction by all means do so, but bear in mind those changes may be focused upon during your examination before the jury and you will need to explain the reason for the change.

Deposition transcripts, sometimes taken years prior, are examined by attorneys looking for positions previously taken by experts that could be used to impeach his or her testimony in current litigations. Some experts have taken one position while assisting in a plaintiff action, such as "lighting is important in deterring criminal activity at night" and years later have testified that lighting was not important as a deterrent. Obviously, the consultant must be consistent in related positions and recognize that the deposition transcript is a permanent record.

The Consultant Testifies in Trial

I trust and respect the U.S. judicial system. Jurors arrive at their decisions based on the facts presented by both sides. Surely, the manner of presentation has some impact, but the facts ultimately tend to speak for themselves. The facts may be put into a better perspective by the testimony of an expert. It is an absolute privilege to be allowed to express an opinion under oath from the witness stand to help the jury in their awesome task of sifting through all the evidence to find the facts, to find the truth.

That privilege never must be abused by shoddy pretrial preparation, or by appearing before the court poorly groomed. We represent the entire security industry, not the defendant or the plaintiff. We are allowed to speak from the box as an exception to the rule, an allowance well thought through because of the need for expert opinion testimony. That makes us a vital component of the judicial process. When you take the stand speak evenly, clearly, and loud enough so all can hear without strain. Answer the questions from both sides with sincerity.

If you have made it to the witness stand as an expert witness, you have come a long way in our industry. As a forensic consultant, you assist the court and jury in their efforts to arrive at a fair judgment, and you bring respect to our industry in general and forensic consulting in particular.

EXAMPLES OF THE TYPES OF CASES SECURITY CONSULTANTS GET INVOLVED WITH

Case #1: Two security officers murder a young man, rape and attempt to murder his girlfriend at a remote telecommunication site. The plaintiff's theory of liability is the officers were negligently hired and negligently supervised.

I was retained by plaintiff's counsel. I determined there were three security officers assigned to the site, each working an 8 hour shift. The "sergeant" worked 8 A.M. to 4 P.M. The other two officers worked the swing and graveyard shifts. The sergeant never made site inspections to see what the other two were doing. The control point, as such, was a security operations desk at the main facility many miles away and the night shift officers were required to phone that desk periodically to ensure they were on the job. Examination of all records disclosed security management's only site visits were during the day shift. No one, ever, checked the site after normal working hours.

The two younger night shift officers soon realized they could do what they wanted, as long as they called the desk from time to time.

On the night in question the swing officer, instead of going home as required, stayed over to visit, drink beer and smoke marijuana with his relief officer and friend. They drove around the extensive site and connecting roadways and happened on a parked car with two teenage lovers. They killed the boy with a knife and pushed him over a cliff. They then raped, sodomized and stabbed the girl numerous times and threw her over the cliff, believing she was dead. She survived, crawled to the road just as the sun was coming up and just as the two officers drove by again. They repeatedly stabbed her again, and again threw her over the edge. The girl again survived and crawled to the road, this time to be discovered by a regular day shift employee.

Aside from the issue of a poor background investigation (but notnecessarily a "negligent" one, as I recall) the control and supervision of these two young officers was negligent, in my opinion.

Case # 2:   A premises liability matter in which a young woman was abducted from a grocery store parking lot, in broad daylight, as she was entering her car, taken to a number of locations including a motel where she was ultimately raped, stabbed and left for dead. The plaintiff's theory of liability was the store provided an inadequate level of security and hence was negligent.

I was retained by the law firm defending the grocery company. After reviewing the history of incidents on the premises, the history of crime in that part of the community, the number of customers, the store's policy of requiring uniformed employees to assist every customer out to their autos with their groceries, the security officers' assignment schedule, the testimony and statements of the two abductors as to the brief periods of time they had been in that parking lot prior to their spontaneous decision to abduct her, I concluded the store was not negligent nor were they responsible for this terrible crime.

Interestingly, the security expert for the plaintiff was of the opinion there should have been a security officer assigned to that lot. I, for one, would never have recommended an officer be assigned to that lot during morning and afternoon hours.

Case # 3:   A premises liability case in which a young mother was abducted from in front of a grocery store at night and that store was located in a strip center. The woman had parked directly in front of the store for the purpose of renting a carpet shampooer. A boxboy carried the shampooer to the rear of her car and wanted to place it in her trunk. She told him she would do it and busied herself with putting her two little children in the car. As she was so engaged a man approached her, put an object in her side and told her to get in the car from the passenger side. Out of fear for her children she complied. He followed her in, closing the door. She was instructed to back out, running over the shampooer. A witness honked her horn continually to catch the victim's attention, in an attempt to avert the destruction of the machine, but the witness had no idea an abduction was occurring. The lot was relatively active and the location of the car in question was well illuminated. The woman was forced to drive to a remote location and was raped in front of her children. I was retained by the victim's attorney to evaluate the security that was provided. The theory of liability was that the store personnel should have reacted to all the honking of the horn and the shopping center security officer was not doing his job.

After reviewing all available data and personally inspecting the property I determined that the security officer was indeed doing his patrols, those patrols were being properly recorded, per the post orders, by an electronic patrol supervisory system and indeed that very security officer within minutes prior to the abduction was leaning down talking to two deputy sheriffs in their patrol vehicle there in the center. I further decided that even if some employee had come out of the store to see why someone was honking, such person would not have understood the dynamics of the event and would not nor could not intervene. As a result, I informed my client I felt there was no negligence and would be unable to serve as their expert witness. My client was disappointed, to say the least, but was undaunted and went out and retained another consultant, in hopes of finding one that would be supportive of their theory.

As these three brief scenarios suggest, this is fascinating and challenging work and in some of these matters, literally millions of dollars are at stake. I would like to conclude by saying, in view of that, that only those with the highest of ethics and qualifications should be allowed to engage in this work. Regrettably this is not the case.

Chapter 11

Ethics in Consulting

Ethics has to do with the general nature of morals and the moral choices to be made by an individual in relationship with others. Certainly all security practitioners need to conform to principles of good and moral conduct, but where and what are those principles? In 1983 over 2,000 men and women identified themselves to *Security World* magazine as security consultants, and that number continues to inch up, but by what standards do they abide? How could it be that literally hundreds of men and women moved throughout our business and industrial communities, accessing confidential, secret, and sensitive proprietary data with no universally accepted Code of Conduct?

Security consultants had no such code until the formation of the International Association of Professional Security Consultants (IAPSC). That newly formed group, recognizing the need for standards of conduct, looked to the Institute of Management Consultants and, with that organization's permission, liberally adopted from their Code of Professional Conduct. The objective of embracing a Code of Professional Conduct was to signify members' willingness to assume an obligation of self-discipline above and beyond requirements of the law. Thus, it notifies clients and prospective clients that members intend to maintain a high level of ethics and professional service, a service of genuine integrity.

The provider of security consulting services, at the very least, should:

1. Place the interest of clients and prospective clients ahead of their own interests.
2. Hold the affairs of their clients in strict confidence.
3. Strive continuously to improve and enhance their professional knowledge and skills.
4. Uphold the honor and dignity of the security profession, in general, and the consulting profession specifically.
5. Maintain the highest standards of personal conduct.

GENERAL STANDARDS FOR CONSULTANTS

In 1984 the IAPSC adopted twenty-nine articles of conduct, in four categories. These were the very first codified rules of ethics ever set down for security consultants, and they clearly delineate all the major points of concern for this profession:

Serving the Client: Basic Responsibilities
1. At all times place the interests of clients ahead of their own and serve their clients with integrity and competence.
2. Assume an independent position with the client, making certain that advice to clients is based on impartial consideration of all pertinent facts and responsible opinions.
3. Guard as confidential all information concerning the affairs of a client that is gathered during the course of the professional assignment.
4. The consultant will not take personal, financial, or other advantage of material or inside information resulting from their professional relationship with clients; nor will the consultant provide the basis on which others might take such advantage.
5. Not serve two or more competing clients in areas of vital interest without informing each client.
6. Inform clients of any special relationships or circumstances of interests that might influence their judgment or impair their objectivity.

Serving the Client: Arrangements
7. Shall, before accepting an assignment, confer with the client in sufficient detail and gather sufficient facts to gain an adequate understanding of the problem, the scope of study needed to solve it, and the possible benefits that may accrue for the client. The preliminary exploration will be conducted confidentially on terms and conditions agreed upon by the consultant and the prospective client.
8. Accept only assignments for which they believe they are qualified. Consultants will recommend that other professionals be retained whenever their special knowledge and skills are needed by the client.
9. Consultants will only accept assignments they believe will prove beneficial to the client.
10. Consultants will not serve a client under terms or conditions that might impair their objectivity, independence, or integrity; they will reserve the right to withdraw if conditions beyond their control develop in a manner that would interfere with the successful conduct and completion of the assignment.
11. Consultants will not accept an assignment of such limited scope that they cannot serve the client effectively.
12. Consultants will present their qualifications for serving a client solely in terms of their competence, experience, and standing.
13. Perform each assignment on an individualized basis and develop recommendations designed specifically for the solution of each client's problems.
14. If conditions change during an assignment, the consultant will discuss with the client any changes in the objectives, scope, and approach or other aspects of the engagement and obtain the client's agreement to such changes before

taking action on them. Unless the circumstances make it unnecessary, they will confirm these in writing.

Serving the Client: Fees

15. Members will not charge more than a reasonable fee. Determination of the reasonableness of a fee will be based upon: the nature of the services performed; the time required; the consultant's experience, ability, and reputation; the degree of responsibility assumed; and the benefits that accrued to the client.

16. Wherever feasible, the consultant will agree with the client in advance on the fee or fee basis.

17. The valuation of services and the procedures by which charges are made are matters of individual preference and are based upon agreement between the consultant and the client. However, the pricing and charging practices should not serve to impair the independent status or objectivity of professional judgments of the consultant, or contribute to a conflict of interest with the client.

18. Members will neither accept nor pay fees or commissions to others for client referrals, or enter into any arrangement for franchising their practice to others; provided, however, that a member may agree with one or more other qualified consultants as to sharing of any fee on a basis reasonably commensurate with the relative values of the services performed.

19. Members will not accept fees, commissions, or other valuable considerations from individuals or organizations whose equipment, supplies, or services they might recommend in the course of their service to clients.

Professional Practices

20. Strive continuously to advance and protect the standards of the security consulting profession.

21. Members will not affiliate or work with any consultant who does not adhere to the standards represented by this Code of Professional Conduct.

22. Consultants recognize their responsibilities to the public interest and to their profession to contribute to the development and understanding of better ways to protect corporations, governmental organizations, the legal profession, and other institutions in our society.

23. Members recognize their responsibility to the profession to share with their colleagues the methods and techniques they utilize in serving clients.

24. Members will not knowingly, without their permission, use proprietary data, procedures, materials, or techniques that other security consultants have developed but not released for public use.

25. Members will not accept an assignment from a client while another security consultant is serving that client unless they are assured, and can satisfy themselves, that any conflict between the two engagements is recognized by, and has the consent of, the client.

26. Members will not endeavor to displace another security consultant once they have knowledge that the client has made a commitment to the other consultant.
27. Consultant will review for a client the work of another security consultant currently engaged by the client only with the other consultant's knowledge, provided that the client consents to the disclosure.
28. Members will strive to avoid not only professional improprieties but also the appearance of improprieties.
29. Consultants may not be convicted of any felony or misdemeanor involving moral turpitude and retain membership in the Association.

STANDARDS FOR FORENSIC CONSULTING

In addition to these, the following ten articles, recommended by Dr. Robert Gallati, address a code of conduct that specifically pertains to the field of forensic work:

1. Members testifying will respond with the truth, the whole truth, and nothing but the truth to appropriate questions.
2. Members will not exaggerate their qualifications in order to have the court, or others, accept them as expert witnesses.
3. Members will not conceal any relevant facts that bear upon their degree of expertise in specific matters concerning their testimony as experts.
4. Members will not discuss pending litigation with anyone, except as approved by the client.
5. Members, when providing expert opinion, will be objective, fair, impartial, and consistent.
6. Members who have been previously subjected to effective cross-examination will disclose this to the client and alert such client to the consultant's points of possible vulnerability in the case at hand.
7. Members are entitled to reasonable fees for professional services as an expert witness; however, any such fees will never be contingent upon the outcome of the case.
8. Members will, if feasible, consent to accept court appointment as an expert at the request of the judiciary.
9. Members, in rendering their expertise in our judicial system, always will be conscious of their dedication to just verdicts.
10. Members, when testifying, will carefully avoid assuming an adversarial approach, or appearing to assume such an approach; for justice requires that the professional security consultant should consider himself or herself neutrally, with no personal interest in the outcome of the case.

Gallati's above ten recommendations are just that: a list of suggestions. I include them as well as the preceding twenty-nine, knowing they all may evolve and be

---

CONSULTING SECURITY AGREEMENT -- JOINT CERTIFICATION

_____ **of** _____
                NAME   STREET ADDRESS

_____ Consultant, and The Corpo-
        CITY/STATE/ZIP CODE

ration (hereinafter called "Contractor"), hereby certify and agree as follows:

(1) Classified information shall not be removed physically from the premises of the Contractor.

(2) Performance of the contract shall be accomplished on the premises of the Contractor,

(3) The Consultant and all certifying employees shall not disclose classified information to unauthorized persons.

_____
          CONSULTANT

_____
             DATE

By: _____

_____
          DATE

FIGURE 11–1   *Nondisclosure agreement (reprinted with permission of The Meritt Company).*

refined. But they are of such fundamental importance to the consulting profession that they cannot be excluded from this work. Without these thirty-nine articles of "faith," what is out there in terms of professional and moral guidelines for the consultant?

Not only do practicing consultants have an abiding concern about the ethics in their profession, so do clients. Clients often will require agreements of nondisclosure and conflict-of-interest statements signed by consultants (see Figures 11–1 and

---

PROTECTION OF ASSETS

CONFLICT OF INTEREST STATEMENT

The undersigned warrants that, to the best of the undersigned consultant's knowledge and belief, and except otherwise disclosed, there are no relevant facts which could give rise to an organizational conflict of interest and that the undersigned consultant has disclosed all relevant information.

The undersigned agrees, that if an organizational conflict of interest is discovered, an immediate and full disclosure in writing shall be made to the Contracting Officer which shall include a description of the action which the undersigned has taken or proposes to take to avoid or mitigate such conflicts.

Date_____

Signature of Consultant

FIGURE 11–2   *Conflict-of-interest statement (reprinted with permission of The Meritt Company).*

11–2). Yet, the signature on an agreement is only as binding as the morality of the person who affixes it to the document. So, the Code of Professional Conduct can be compared to an oath of office, or the physician's Hippocratic oath—these oaths of ethical professional behavior work only as well as we apply them.

Appendix B is a copy of an agreement for consulting services that was included in the *Protection of Assets Manual*, in a chapter on consultants. The agreement includes, among other important factors, the issue of ethics. Paragraph 6, Professional Standards, read as follows:

> Consultant agrees that the work performed hereunder will represent her or his best efforts and will be of the highest professional standards and quality.

I underscore *highest professional standards*. To what standards was the author or designer of the agreement referring? To my knowledge, other than the IAPSC's code and what has been presented in this chapter, none exist for consultants in the security industry.

This issue of and concern about ethics is not some vague idealism which consultants wrap themselves in as an enhancement to marketing. The truth is security consultants are perceived as a model of knowledge and *honesty*. Most professions are known or suspected to have a dark side. Most have heard of doctors and lawyers who have engaged in unethical or unscrupulous conduct. Consultants, for the most part, particularly security consultants are really the last bastion of unquestioned honesty. That is our image. And the IAPSC is committed to safeguard that perception.

Chapter 12

The Computer as an Aid to Consulting

My last survey of IAPSC (albeit less than half the membership) disclosed that 83% of those surveyed utilized the personal computer in their practice. Such users are strident in their support of the particular hardware they use and the software programs they rely on in their individual practices. Users agree the computer is no longer a novelty or nicety, but an operating necessity.

For a variety of perspectives, I asked five of my colleagues to contribute to this topic by preparing a few words about a given aspect of their use of the computer.

Kevin Murray, Murray Associates, of Clinton, NJ, writes:

My First Employee

It's 6:00 A.M. Mac wakes up.

- Task one . . . Check FAXSTF® program for overnight faxes . . . process, and send them to the printer with instructions to begin printing at 8:50 A.M. FAXSTF® also transmits our sales literature, client security bulletins and newsletters. Instantly or overnight when phone rates are lowest. High resolution transmissions right from the computer are sharp and clear. Clients are impressed.
- Task two . . . Open Now Up-to-Date®, our office calendar. Sort today's appointments, reminders, calls, jobs, and meetings. Send daily *to-do list* to the printer. Little falls through the cracks. Promises are kept. Clients are impressed.
- Task three . . . Open FileMaker Pro®, a database program. Sort and crunch the accounting file. Report . . . Year-to-date billing, breakdown of expenses and fees, and this month's activity. Plot the trends. Tell us how we are doing. Make sure we know promptly. Business decisions and plans are intrinsically tied to client satisfaction.
- Task four . . . Collections. FileMaker Pro sorts through client invoices. Three days after a report and invoice is sent (via FedEx), a follow-up phone call is scheduled. On day fifteen a thank you note and custom china coffee cup are scheduled to be sent. If the invoice has not been paid by day 35 (a rare occurrence) the account is flagged for action that day. The type of action taken will vary depending upon the client, and their previous payment record. Clients are impressed with the attention . . . and pay their bills.

It's 6:08 A.M. I'm still at home—asleep—but a lot of my work has already been done.

During the day my Mac and its two sister computers will continue to work. Accounting, payroll, publishing-on-demand, graphic artwork production, marketing, faxing, report writing, electronic photography, FedEx tracking and even a pinball game.

When I began Murray Associates—an electronic eavesdropping detection firm—I had a choice to make. Buy an expensive memory typewriter, or buy *into* an unproved, new technology—the personal computer. In 1980 the cost was approximately the same either way. I bought an Apple computer. Best business decision I ever made.

Jack Case, John D. Case & Associates, Del Mar, CA, focused specifically on the laptop, as follows:

The Laptop Computer

Since time is literally money to a consultant, every effort should be made to avoid "dead time" during travel and other non-office activities. Your time in the office should be geared to continually marketing your services and avoidance of routine or non-direct income activities during this period. Developing contact lists, sending faxes, writing reports, scheduling tasks, and expense tracking are only a few examples of activities that can be accomplished outside of the office with a laptop computer.

As a security consultant, imaging yourself in the following situations:

- You have conducted a security survey and returned to your motel room to await your flight back home the following morning. Just think what an advantage it would be to write your report that night and on the flight.
- You are on the road, check your messages and find a potential client has left an urgent message for you to send your resume or other information needed to award the engagement. With a laptop computer, you could fax this information within minutes from a phone.
- You are on location and your client calls a meeting for the following morning to discuss your findings or determine if the scope of your engagement should be expanded to cover additional areas. Your laptop can have the capability of creating overhead transparencies to create a professional and impressive presentation that night and enhance your chances to get additional business.
- You find yourself on the road a great deal and tend to procrastinate putting bills out when you finally get back to the office. With a time accounting program on your laptop, you could enter your time while in the field and send bills out within minutes of returning to your office.

The introduction of a multitude of practical business software programs allows even the most novice computer user to accomplish these and other tasks away from the office. Since time is money to you, the laptop computer is an indispensable tool to extend your working day to become more efficient, competitive, and responsible to your clients.

Whereas Kevin Murray referred to his Mac as his "First Employee," Ira S. Somerson, Loss Management Consultants, Inc., Plymouth Meeting, PA, talks about a "Best Friend":

Notebooks Are a Consultant's Best Friend

PC workstations, as we know and love them, have been around since 1985. They have so changed our workplace that it seems they have actually been here longer. But it was not until the evolution of the "laptop" and its successor the "notebook" that security management consultants significantly benefited from this technology.

Consultants are like worker bees. They are constantly on the move, taking ideas from one place to another and replanting them. What has always distinguished an excellent consultant was their ability to *communicate* ideas and to *facilitate* necessary change. Portable data communications, wordprocessing, relational databases, and presentation software packages just make a good communicator all the better. A look at four software concepts crystallizes the value-added benefits of notebooks:

- **Word Processing:** Those who used typewriters before wordprocessing understand the time saved in preparing proposals, opinions, reports, etc. If a consultant learns to be a good typist with a wordprocessor and then transfers this skill to a notebook, their office literally goes where they go. With the memory capacity now available on a notebook's hard drive, consultants can literally carry their client's entire correspondence file under their arm. There are obvious cosmetic benefits to work produced by wordprocessing, but a consultant's productivity and information resources grow exponentially when they use notebooks on the road.
- **Presentation (Graphics) Software:** The skills of communicating and facilitating take on a whole new meaning when presentations are designed and prepared by your notebook's presentation software. For example, after conducting a risk assessment at your client's facility, the consultant sits down and prepares overhead transparencies, 35 mm slides, or even an animated visual presentation of their findings. Still photographs can be developed and scanned into your program (or directly scanned from a special still or video camera without developing) and used with your presentation. All of these methodologies can be ready the same day as your survey for presentation to management or the client's focus group. If your client's computer facilities are not available to do this, 24 hour printing, copying, and computer facilities exist in most cities that provide these support services quite reasonably. These visuals can later be transferred into the wordprocessing program and made part of the final report or opinion.
- **Data Communications:** When a consultant can query his or her office computer system any time of day or night, conduct extensive on-line research with a multitude of data services, communicate interactively with other computer users, and fax or deliver extensive data to their clients anywhere in the world from their notebook; the only limitation to their portability is the availability of a phone line. As newer systems are now being designed with cellular telephones built into the notebooks, even this limitation will dissolve into being within acceptable distance to the nearest communications cell. Privacy and information security issues still remain, but these problems are being managed (not economically yet) with data communications security technology.
- **Relational Databases:** The use of relational databases has long been the mainstay of technical consulting, but security management consultants have only recently begun to take advantage of this technology. Consultants whose practices have survived many years realize that they are the custodians of significant data. How these data are retrieved, analyzed, and reused goes directly to the issue of a

consultant's worth to their clients. Here are some very useful ways to use a relational database:

— Each time you do work for a client, load all relational data about the client and the type of consulting services you provided. This will be extremely useful in constructing client lists, avoiding conflicts of interest, and listing clients by types of industry and services you rendered. Does a prospective client want to know if you have served their industry type or if the type of service they want was performed by you previously and with whom? If your notebook is with you, you will know in seconds! There is no longer a reason to wait until you get back to the office and then learn that your impatient prospect went to someone else. How often have you clipped an article and then not been able to find it when you needed it months or years later? Construct a reference index database by assigning each article (book, monograph, etc.) a reference number. Before numerically filing the reference, load all relational data about the reference into your database (e.g., source, author, date, annotation of reference contents, keyword sort field, etc.). This would, for example, permit you to retrieve all materials you have saved on "workplace violence" or "information security," etc. When you receive your next assignment, you are ready to retrieve and send to your client independent references to support project recommendations, opinions, etc. With today's high speed scanning equipment, consultants can scan important reference materials for an assignment before leaving the office. These data can be printed to hard copy or reviewed on the notebook at the client's facility.

There are, of course, other important uses for your notebook, but those that define the consultant's professionalism, communication and facilitation skills, and ability to be productive stand out most prominently. The list of benefits will only grow with technological developments. Future clients will identify with consultants conversant with these technologies. Consultants would serve themselves well to get on board now and acclimate themselves. Surely if they do not, others will swiftly pass them by.

Bill Wilson, Wilson Security, Lake Elsinor, CA, says:

The use of a computer in my business is essential. From maintaining financial data, doing spreadsheet analysis and sending out marketing material, it has become an integral part of my practice.

One of the major projects was to create a database of information. This database allows me to continue adding information along with cataloging entries. For example, in my file I have clients, potential clients, friends, vendors, different business categories for clients, referrals, dates of birth, last contact, etc. I have the ability to target certain segments for business. I can select all drug industry contacts or I can select drug manufacturers only. I can select a list of all those who get my newsletter. Publishing a monthly newsletter would be impossible without a computer.

I can select only those who have given me a referral for business. This allows me to periodically thank them and also ask for more referrals. I can select individuals that I have not contacted in the last 90 days. This keeps me in contact with those who might bring me business or potential clients.

I send out a lot of cards. I try to stay in touch with many people. When I send a card, the database automatically identifies which card I sent and the date. This allows

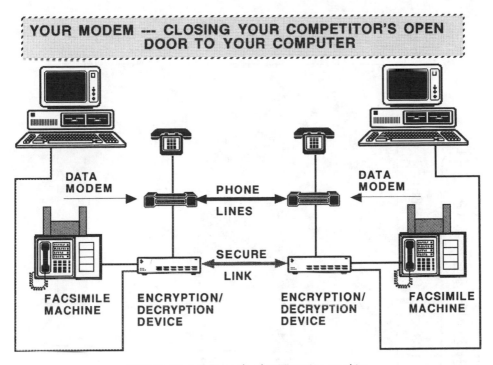

YOUR MODEM --- CLOSING YOUR COMPETITOR'S OPEN DOOR TO YOUR COMPUTER

FIGURE 12-1 *Example of presentation graphics.*

me to send different cards and not have my cards become routine. I can have the database notify me of all birthdays in the next 30 days. I have a place for spouse's name, kids' names, secretary's name, etc. I have a category for Christmas cards.

I can merge the data in my database with a wordprocessing file. This allows me to send a personal letter to any group of individuals I desire. I can send a promotional letter to wholesale drug company presidents only. Or I can send promotional material to hospital presidents or drug manufacturing presidents only.

Ray Chambers, Assets Protection Systems Associates, Inc., Largo, FL, shares the bottom line aspects of his use of the computer with actual examples of some graphic illustrations, as evidenced in Figures 12-1, 12-2, and 12-3.

Ray, a security management consultant for the past eleven years, has made extensive use of Macintosh computer systems throughout his practice, and is currently on his third upgraded system. The current system in use is a Macintosh Quadra 650 system with a Radius Precision Color monitor, Color-One Scanner, and a Hewlett-Packard, HP 650C Desk Writer ink-jet color printer. This is backed up by a Macintosh SE and TI microlaser printer, as well as a Macintosh PowerBook 170 and portable printer for field use. Chambers uses the computer for all of the usual administrative functions in his practice, as well as financial accounting, reports to clients, and operational statistical analysis.

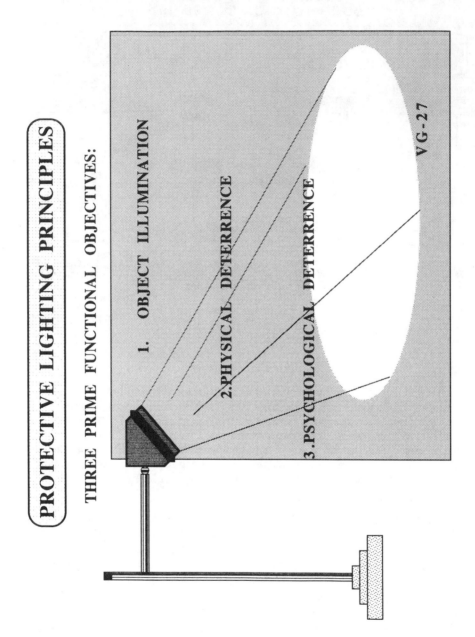

PROTECTIVE LIGHTING PRINCIPLES

THREE PRIME FUNCTIONAL OBJECTIVES:

1. OBJECT ILLUMINATION
2. PHYSICAL DETERRENCE
3. PSYCHOLOGICAL DETERRENCE

VG-27

FIGURE 12–2 *Example of presentation graphics.*

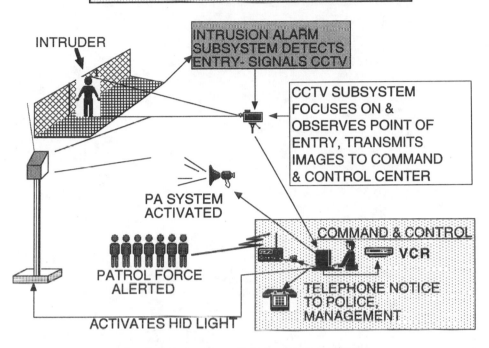

FIGURE 12–3 *Example of presentation graphics.*

Chambers considers the computer systems at his disposal as indispensable elements of his practice.

Recently, he was asked by a client to create and deliver a two-day seminar on industrial security for a foreign audience of corporate executives and security managers.

The entire program, including visuals, had to be created within $2\frac{1}{2}$ months. Chambers' primary computer system enabled him to produce an eighty-page outline and text, as well as 120 color-enhanced, graphic-illustrated visual transparencies, to reinforce the oral presentation, easily within the imposed time constraints. The program was produced entirely in-house, at minimal cost (less than $200 in outlay for materials). It is estimated that if Chambers had relied upon outside production sources, the cost would have approximated $3,000. This figure, for a single project approximates 55% of the retail cost of the primary computer system Chambers uses. Think about the ROI (return on investment) implications of those numbers, as well as those in the next paragraph!

Although Chambers regards the seminar program primarily as a marketing tool to potentially exploit a burgeoning Latin-American market for security management consulting, the seminar program may potentially provide income in excess of $10,000, which in itself provides more than 150% return on investment in the primary computer system which he uses in his practice.

Chapter 13

The Need for Professional Growth

The Origin of the International Association of Professional Security Consultants

I started my consulting practice in late 1979 and by 1982 it became apparent to me that I was operating in a vacuum. I was talking to the walls of my office. I was growing in terms of reputation, engagements, and income but I was a professional satellite, orbiting alone with no meaningful or intellectual contact or stimuli with my consulting peers.

I contacted the headquarters of the American Society for Industrial Security and talked to the executive director, suggesting the possible creation of a standing committee for security consultants, but after a number of internal consultations the idea was rejected.

I approached the editor of *Security World* magazine, the forerunner of today's *Security Magazine*, and shared with him my vision of a security consultant's organization. That call resulted in the magazine, working with the International Security Conference exhibits/seminars, accommodating the needed publicity and facilities for consultants to come together and discuss the possibility of forming an association. I held meetings during 1983 in Los Angeles, Chicago and New York. Several hundred "consultants" attended these meetings and the two key questions that were addressed were: 1) is there a need for an association? and if so 2) what qualifications would be required for membership?

There was an overwhelming agreement that an association was needed, but a sharp debate arose, in each meeting, about membership and membership restrictions. On one hand there were those who either engaged in "turn-key" consulting work, i.e., sold the client the hardware specified in the recommendations, and those who were private investigators who "consulted" when the opportunity presented itself. The opposing group, always smaller in number, but obviously (to me) more professional, opted for the "purist" approach, i.e., pure or exclusive consultants who did not sell anything other than their wisdom, experience, and advice. I was persuaded by the logic of the latter group and made notes on the back of business cards I collected at each of these meetings.

From those cards I invited some twenty consultants across the country to come together in a founding meeting at the Barneby Hotel in Los Angeles in early January 1984. Eighteen men came together then, for two days, and founded the International Association of Professional Security Consultants (IAPSC). It was an inspiring experience to work and share with my unique peers, something I knew would fill that professional vacuum. At last, a vehicle for professional growth as a consultant!

The IAPSC

This association really has three missions:

1. To provide to business and industry a single source of truly professional, pre-screen consultants whose sole purpose is to provide a quality consulting service instead of pursuing some other agenda, such as selling equipment or other services.
2. To provide a forum for truly professional consultants for their business and professional growth, and to upgrade themselves.
3. To promote, protect, and polish the image of the consultant in our industry.

To explain the advantages of membership in the IAPSC, the only security consultant's organization in existence, the following was published under the heading: Why Should You Join IAPSC?:

> The IAPSC represents the interest of independent consultants in regard to federal and state legislation, codes and standards and other matters of a similar nature.
>
> The Association newsletter serves as a means of communication between members. It contains information that can save money, improve skills and possibly could help in winning contracts.
>
> The annual meeting and seminar is an opportunity to network with your colleagues, exchange information and gain new ideas and information.
>
> The membership directory includes a biography and photo of each member and is distributed to users of consulting services and is provided to those seeking a consultant. Figure 13–1 is a page from that directory.
>
> Through the IAPSC, members often receive free exposure in trade and professional publications.
>
> The IAPSC has identified a relatively low cost Errors and Omissions Insurance, exclusively for security consultants.

Qualifications for Membership

Education: A Baccalaureate or higher degree from an accredited college or university. Eight years of direct, broad security experience may be accepted by the Membership Committee as equivalent on a case-by-case basis.

Charles A. Sennewald, CPP
Security Management Consultant

Charles A. Sennewald & Associates
28004 Lake Meadow Drive
Escondido, California 92026
(619) 749-7527

Year Established: 1979

Services:
   Conducts security surveys to identify organizational and operational strengths and weaknesses in protection and loss prevention programs and makes cost-effective recommendations to cure or reduce deficiencies and maximize committed resources. Assists in security related litigations.

Environments Serviced:
   Retailers, manufacturing facilities, shopping centers, residential complexes, office/high rise buildings, parking facilities (surface, subterranean, multi-level) and security organizations (departments) in any environment.

Experience:
   Prior to establishing his practice as a security management consultant, Mr. Sennewald served 18 years with the Broadway department stores as a security executive. Prior to the Broadway he was Chief of Security for the Claremont Colleges and a Deputy Sheriff with the County of Los Angeles. He earned his B.S. degree in police science at California State University in L.A., where he subsequently lectured for 13 years in security administration. His two books, *Effective Security Management* and *The Process of Investigation* are both used in English-speaking countries around the world in colleges and universities that offer courses in the security/loss prevention field. *Effective Security Management* is today considered a standard in the industry.
   Mr. Sennewald has twice been appointed Security Industry Representative by the U.S. Department of Commerce and in that capacity has served in Sweden, Denmark, Japan, Republic of China and Hong Kong.

Professional Affiliations:
   IAPSC (International Association of Professional Security Consultants: Founder and
      first President)
   ASIS (American Society for Industrial Security)
   ASET (Academy of Security Educators and Trainers)
   Mr. Sennewald is the holder of the professional designation CPP (Certified Protection
      Professional)

FIGURE 13–1   *Individual IAPSC member's page in directory.*

Experience: At least five years of broad security experience in paid positions, demonstrating increasing responsibilities, with at least three years at management or higher levels. No part of this requirement may be used as a substitute for educational requirement.

Certification: The following may be accepted by the Membership Committee in place of the Education qualification:

Certified Protection Professional with at least three years' additional experience. Membership in the bar of any state, commonwealth or country, with at least three years' additional experience.
Other certifications may be accepted at the discretion of the Membership Committee.

Membership Requirements

An *Active Member* shall be a person whose primary working income is derived from providing security advice, information and recommendations to management. The Active Member shall have been engaged in this activity for a minimum of one year prior to the date of the application.

An *Associate Member* shall be a person who meets the above criteria, except that activity does not provide his or her primary working income (e.g., a university professor, a security executive who is doing some part-time consulting or a law enforcement officer who does some consulting work on the side).

The annual meetings of the association focus on the kinds of issues that are of most concern to the membership. Mini-workshop sessions have included such topics as:

- Marketing and selling your service
- Proposal writing
- Sharing examples of reports
- Handling collection problems
- Becoming an expert witness
- Preparing graphics for presentations

Attending these annual meetings, spending time with those who engage in the same kinds of work and problems, who share formally, in sessions, and informally around the pool, only enhances professional growth.

In addition to professional growth, there are unlimited opportunities for the growth of one's consulting practice through networking, sharing projects and referrals: the kinds of things that do not and cannot happen unless you all know one another.

Whereas this book you are now reading is deemed a relatively important contribution to our industry, I personally view the creation of the IAPSC *the* most important contribution I ever made. And interestingly, I have gained as a person and a professional immeasurably as a consequence of my association with the highest quality of individuals in the security industry.

A Publication of the International Association of Professional Security Consultants, Inc.

INDEPENDENT CONSULTANT

March / April 1995   Volume 6 / Number 2

Tampa Hosts the IAPSC 11th Annual Conference

The 11th Annual Conference is scheduled for April 23-26 at the Tradewinds Resort, Tampa Bay/St. Petersburg Beach Area in Florida. This year's program focuses on "Expanding Your Horizons New Options and Opportunities" with topics such as Overview of the Industry, International Community and The Electronic Office, among others. All interested executives, practicing consultants and security professionals are welcome. Call IAPSC at 301-656-2880 if you are interested in attending. ❖

Nominees for IAPSC Board

Thanks to the Nominating Committee consisting of: Robert O. Murphy, CPP (chair), William A. Hawthorne, CPP, R. Bruce Kamm, Gabriel G.J. Saint Vitoux and William S. Wilson, CPP, who developed the slate.

In accordance with the IAPSC bylaws the following nominees were submitted:

President	Mark M. Warrington, CPP
Vice President	Thomas O. Roemer, CPP
Secretary	James H. Clark, CPP
Treasurer	William S. Wilson, CPP

The following persons are nominated for the Board of Directors:
David G. Aggleton, CPP
Ken Braunstein
John D. Case, CPP

Lance R. Foster, CPP, CFE
William A. Hawthorne, CPP
Steven C. Kaufer, CPP
Kevin D. Murray, CPP
Gerald A. O'Rourke, CPP
Robert C. Quigley, CPP
Charles A. Sennewald, CPP, CMC
John R. Smith
Ira S. Somerson, CPP
Robert E. Spiel, JD, CPP

Nomination of an associate member has not been established.

For the officer positions one candidate for each is listed. Our bylaws do not mandate two candidates for each officer position, saying only that not more than two can be nominated. We can call for additional nominations from the floor.

The nominated members are an outstanding group and will well serve the IAPSC. ❖

ASTM Committee May Cease Work On Premises Security

by Jerry V. Wilson, CPP

Almost since inception of the ASTM Committee on Premises Security, there has been discussion at committee meetings regarding whether or not formally adopted "standards" for premises security would be helpful either for crime prevention or to shield premises owners or managers from litigation.

Proponents of standards have argued that much security related crime and subsequent litigation arises from cases where premises owners have failed to conform to basic principles of security, that adoption of consensus standards would be an instrument for informing owners and managers of what is required for proper security, and that owners and managers conforming to the standards would enjoy to that extent a shield from litigation.

Opponents have contended that the field of premises security is too varied in kinds of premises and kinds of risks for there to be consensus on other than very basic principles of security, that these basic standards end up so ambiguously worded that ordinary persons would be uncertain of the meaning, that ASTM standards are unlikely to have wide distribution to those owners and managers without access to equally good or better guidance from their own "industry" associations, and that "standards" will be used by plaintiffs' attorneys as a minimum procedure, to which they will claim that other, more comprehensive security should have been added.

The "Wall Street Journal" [October 19, 1994, B1] discussed the litigation hazards which have resulted from consensus standards adopted by medical peer groups trying to deter malpractice lawsuits. The basic expectations of such standards are, of course, first, that adoption of published standards will insure that all professionals in the field are aware of precisely what is expected of them under certain procedures; and, second, that any practitioner adhering fully to consensus standards in a given procedure is, prima facie, conforming to the 'standard of

Continued on page 3

FIGURE 13-2   *IAPSC newsletter.*

Institute of Management Consultants

Although the IAPSC has indeed provided a meaningful vehicle for professional growth, I felt its limitations in that the membership is exclusively comprised of security people and in my view we could get tunnel vision if we do not broaden our horizons.

Where can one associate with consultants of all disciplines? The answer was clear. The IAPSC had permission from the Institute of Management Consultants (IMC) to liberally borrow from its by-laws and Code of Conduct which had been developed back in its formation in 1968. The IMC services consultants of every conceivable discipline and offers an awesome array of programs aimed at continued growth offered not only at their annual meeting but by various chapters scattered around the country.

The IMC's stated purpose is as follows:

The primary purpose of the Institute of Management Consultants is to assure the public that members possess the ethical standards and the professional competence and independence required for membership and are, therefore, qualified to practice.

More broadly, the goal of the Institute is to help ensure standards which will engender greater public confidence in the management consulting profession. Additional important purposes are:

- to provide opportunities for consultants to improve their technical and consulting skills through specialized training and career development programs
- to gain public recognition for Institute certification and to enhance the reputation of management consulting as a profession.

One must be certified for membership. To achieve this Certified Management Consultant (CMC) certification one must have a minimum of five years' consulting experience, a bachelor's degree, must submit a list of past clients, who are contacted to verify the quality of work, successfully pass an oral examination/interview and a written test.

I earned my CMC in 1992 after identifying that goal as a worthy endeavor and evidence of continuing professional growth, although I was 61 years old at the time. To my knowledge, there are but four security consultants who have their CMC. I pray this chapter stimulates more.

The IMC's *Journal of Management Consulting* is published twice a year and is of superior quality.

Here is a sample of the articles contained in the journal:

- When Consultants are Hired
- Strategy Implementation Hurdles: A Diagnostic Paradigm
- How Changes in Federal Rules Could Affect Management Consultant Expert Witnesses
- To Be or Not to Be ... a Partner
- Critical Factors for Consulting to Small Business

- How to Consult to Government
- Implementing TQM on a Shoestring
- Engagement Fees
- How Do I Go International?
- Establishing Alliances

The IMC's seminar programs are equally stimulating. Following is a sampling of what they have offered to their membership:
Learn how to:

- Overcome roadblocks to successful engagements
- Close sales and handle objections
- Plan and conduct better client interviews
- Write winning proposals
- Facilitate client participation
- Improve profits through effective billing
- Professional referrals
- Borderless consulting
- Consulting fees today

Surely it should be apparent that the successful security management consultant has to be skilled not only in his or her niche specialty of security but must be equally skilled in the art and business of being a consultant. How is that achieved? By pursuing professional growth as a consultant in active participation in such consulting organizations as the IAPSC and IMC—that's how.

Appendix A

Consulting Contract

This sample contract is provided for your convenience and is one of many alternative styles you can use. We suggest that you consult your attorney. We are not providing legal advice and do not recommend this contract as anything but a possible choice.

CONSULTING CONTRACT

This agreement is made as of <u>Date</u> between <u>Your Firm</u> and <u>Your Client.</u>

In the event of a conflict in the provisions of any attachments hereto and the provisions set forth in this agreement, the provisions of such attachments shall govern.

1. *Services.* Consultant agrees to perform for Client the services listed in the Scope of Services section in Exhibit A, attached hereto [see page 134] and executed by both Client and Consultant. Such services are hereinafter refered to as "Services." Client agrees that consultant shall have ready access to Client's staff and resources as necessary to perform the Consultant's services provided for by this contract.

2. *Rate of Payment for Services.* Client agrees to pay Consultant for Services in accordance with the schedule contained in Exhibit B [see page 134] attached hereto and executed by both Client and Consultant.

3. *Reimbursement for Expenses.* Consultant shall be reimbursed by Client for all reasonable expenses incurred by Consultant in the performance of Services, including, but not limited to, travel expenses of Consultant and Consultant's staff, long distance telephone calls, and supplies.

4. *Invoicing.* Client shall pay the amounts agreed to herein upon receipt of invoices which shall be sent by, and client shall pay the amount of such invoices to, Consultant. Invoices are sent monthly for work performed in the month. A final invoice is submitted upon completion of the project.

5. *Confidential Information.* Each party hereto ("Such Party") shall hold in trust for the other party hereto ("Such Other Party"), and shall not disclose to any nonparty to the agreement any confidential information of Such Other Party. Confidential information is information which relates to Such Other Party's

security, operations, trade secrets, or business affairs, but does not include information which is generally known or easily ascertainable by nonparties of ordinary skill.

6. *Staff.* Neither Consultant nor Consultant's staff is or shall be deemed to be employees of Client. Consultant shall take appropriate measures to insure that its staff who perform Services are competent to do so and that they do not breach Section 5 hereof. Consultant and staff are independent contractors. Consultant assumes full responsibility for payment of any taxes due on money received hereunder. Client will not make any deductions for taxes.

7. *Use of Work Product.* Consultant and Client agree that Client shall have nonexclusive ownership of the deliverable products described in Exhibit A and the ideas embodied therein. The Consultant's notes and a file copy of all reports, blueprints, drawings, or other products in written, computer media, or other format shall be retained in a secure manner by the Consultant.

8. *Client Representative.* The following individual, _____ , shall represent the Client during the performance of this contract with respect to the services and deliverables as defined herein and has authority to execute written modifications of additions to this contract as defined in Section 13.

9. *Independent Status.* The Consultant is an independent consultant and does not represent or sell any product or service or benefit from any recommendation made herein.

Limited Warranty

10. *Liability.* Consultant warrants to Client that the material, analysis, data, programs, and services to be delivered or rendered hereunder will be of the kind and quality designated and will be performed by qualified personnel. Special requirements for format or standards to be followed shall be attached as an additional Exhibit and executed by both Client and Consultant. Consultant makes no other warranties, whether written, oral, or implied, including without limitation warranty or fitness for purpose or merchantability. In no event shall Consultant be liable for special or consequential damages, in either contract or tort, whether or not the possibility of such damages has been disclosed to Consultant in advance or could have been reasonably foreseen by Consultant and, in the event this limitation of damages is held unenforceable, then the parties agree that by reason of the difficulty in foreseeing possible damages, all liability to client shall be limited to One Hundred Dollars ($100.00) as liquidated damages and not as penalty.

The Client fully understands that the Consultant is not an insurer and cannot insure the protection of the facility or its contents, employees, visitors, or others. The protection of a public facility or private institution such as the Client's facility cannot be insured without extraordinary measures. The Client agrees that the Consultant is to recommend security measures and devices which are reasonable in nature, and the lack of additional recommendations will not be construed as errors or omissions of the Consultant.

11. *Complete Agreement.* This agreement contains the entire agreement between the parties hereto with respect to the matters covered herein. No other agreements, representations, warranties, or other matters, oral or written, purportedly agreed to or represented by or on behalf of Consultant by any of Consultant's employees or agents, or contained in any sales materials or brochures, shall be deemed to bind the parties hereto with respect to the subject matter hereof. Client acknowledges to be entering into this Agreement solely on the basis of the representations contained hereon. This agreement supersedes all prior proposals, agreements, understandings, representations, and conditions.

12. *Applicable Law.* Consultant shall comply with all applicable laws in performing Services but shall be held harmless for violation of any governmental procurement regulation to which it may be subject, but to which reference is not made in Exhibit A. This Agreement shall be construed in accordance with the laws of the State indicated by the Consultant's address.

13. *Scope of Agreement.* If the scope of any of the provisions of the Agreement is too broad in any respect whatsoever to permit enforcement to its full extent, then such provisions shall be enforced to the maximum extent permitted by law, and the parties hereto consent and agree that such scope may be judicially modified accordingly and that the whole of such provisions of this Agreement shall not thereby fail, but that the scope of such provisions shall be curtailed only to the extent necessary to conform to law.

14. *Additional Work.* After receipt of an order that adds to the Services, Consultant may, at her or his discretion, take reasonable action and expend reasonable amounts of time and money based on such order. Client agrees to pay and reimburse Consultant for such action and expenditure as set forth in Exhibit B of this Agreement for payments and reimbursements related to Services.

15. *Notices.*

(i) Notices to Client should be sent to:_____

(ii) Notices to Consultant should be sent to:_____

16. *Assignment.* This Agreement may not be assigned by either party, without the prior written consent of the other party. Except for the prohibition on assignment contained in the preceding sentence, this Agreement shall be binding upon and inure to the benefit of the heirs, successors, and assigns of the parties hereto. Nothing in this provision prohibits the Consultant from utilizing the services of a qualified specialist-associate.

IN WITNESS WHEREOF, the parties hereto have signed this Agreement as of the date first above written.

_____   _____
CLIENT (Title)   Date

_____   _____
CONSULTANT (Title)   Date

EXHIBIT A: SCOPE OF SERVICES

The Consultant agrees to perform the following services for the Client pursuant to the Contract affixed hereto:

List what you intend to do for the client here so as to define the scope of services. If you intend to provide a report, say so.

_____

_____

_____

_____

We hereby accept the Scope of Services as herein described.

_____	_____
Client (Title)	Date

_____	_____
Consultant (Title)	Date

EXHIBIT B: RATE OF PAYMENT

The work outlined in Exhibit A: Scope of Services will be performed for a total fee not to exceed $_____, excluding expenses. Work will be billed at the rate of $_____ per hour for work performed within 25 miles of the main office of the Consultant and a rate of $_____ per hour for work performed beyond 25 miles of the main office of the Consultant.

Specification writing will be performed at a rate of $_____ per hour regardless of where the work occurs.

Travel time is billed at the out-of-town rate.

Expenses are actual, tourist-class rates. Effort is made to obtain the lowest reasonable air fare using a major carrier. The Client recognizes that air fares vary greatly and the lowest fares require advance reservations.

The Client agrees to pay any fee or service charge incurred by the Consultant as a result of any cancellation of air or hotel reservations or other accommodations when the cancellation is at the request of the Client or made necessary for the convenience of the Client. This includes cancellation of air reservations made necessary by the weather at the Client's airport.

The Client agrees to pay reasonable meal and lodging costs, ground transportation costs, and other similar expenses. Client will, if necessary for the project, provide at least one set of architectural blueline prints and three sets of reduced floor plans. If the reproduction of blueline prints is necessary for the project, the Client authorizes the Consultant to produce vellums, cepias, or other copies as necessary and to pay the cost of the reproduction.

Mailing and parcel costs will be the responsibility of the Client.

The following fees and expenses are due and payable in advance:

_____

Invoices are mailed at the end of the month for work performed in that month and are due and payable immediately. A final invoice is submitted upon completion of the project or project phase.

We accept the above terms and rate of payment:

_____   _____

Client (Title)   Date

_____   _____

Consultant (Title)   Date

Appendix B

Professional Services Agreement

PROFESSIONAL SERVICES AGREEMENT

AGREEMENT, made as of _____, by _____, an individual, hereinafter referred to as the "Consultant," and _____, a company.

WITNESSETH:

WHEREAS Company and Consultant desire to enter into an agreement for the performance by Consultant of professional services in connection with programs of research and development and other activities of Company.

NOW, THEREFORE, in consideration of the premises and of the mutual promises herein, the parties hereto agree as follows:

1. RETAINER-TERM. This agreement is made with Consultant as an independent contractor and not as an employee of Company. The Company hereby retains Consultant and Consultant agrees to perform professional services for the Company commencing the date set forth above and concluding _____ _____.

2. STATEMENT OF WORK. The work described in the attachment hereto entitled "Scope of Work" and incorporated herein shall be performed by Consultant as requested from time to time by Company, at such place or places as shall be mutually agreeable.

3. PAYMENT. (a) Company shall pay Consultant at the rate of _____ _____ for each _____ spent on the work hereunder during the terms of this agreement. Unless and until revised by a written amendment to this Agreement, Company shall not be obligated to Consultant and Consultant shall not be entitled to payment from Company for more than _____ days/hours. Time spent in travel hereunder during normal working hours or otherwise, if requested by Company, shall be paid for at the above rate. (b) Company shall pay or reimburse Consultant for travel and other appropriate expenses incurred in the performance of work hereunder in accordance with the attachment hereto entitled: "Consultant Expense."

4. PATENT RIGHTS. Consultant will disclose promptly to Company all ideas, inventions, discoveries, and improvements, hereafter referred to as "Subject Inventions," whether or not patentable, relating to the work hereunder which are conceived or first reduced to practice by Consultant in the performance of the work under this agreement. Consultant agrees to keep a written record of technical activities and that all such records and such Subject Inventions shall become the sole property of Company. During or subsequent to the period of this agreement, Consultant will execute and deliver to Company all such documents and take such other action as may be reasonably required by Company to assist it in obtaining patents and vesting in the Company or its designee title to said Subject Inventions; except, however, that as to Subject Inventions not conceived but first reduced to practice hereunder, Consultant's obligations shall be only to the extent that such actions may be made by Consultant without incurring liability to others solely because of such actions.

5. COPYRIGHTS. Consultant agrees that all writings produced by Consultant under this agreement shall be the sole property of Company, and Company shall have exclusive right to copyright such writings in any country or countries; however, Company will make its best efforts to grant a nonexclusive right to Consultant to publish such writings when circumstances, including security regulations, will permit.

6. PROFESSIONAL STANDARDS. Consultant agrees that the work performed hereunder will represent the best efforts and will be of the highest professional standards and quality.

7. SECURITY. Company agrees to apprise Consultant of any information or items made available hereunder to Consultant which are Classified or Restricted Data, and Consultant agrees to comply with the security requirements imposed with respect thereto by the United States Government or the Company. If it becomes necessary for Consultant to store classified material at Consultant's place of business, other than the Company, a facility clearance will be required. In this event, Consultant agrees to enter into a security agreement with the Department of Defense and to maintain a system of security controls in accordance with the requirements set forth in "Department of Defense Industrial Security Manual for Safeguarding Classified Security Information." Consultant further agrees that any classified material furnished by the Company will be immediately returned to the Company upon termination of either the security agreement or this Professional Services Agreement.

8. RISK OF LOSS. Consultant assumes all risk of personal injury, and all risk of damage to or loss of personal property furnished by Consultant's office.

9. PRIVILEGED OR PROPRIETARY INFORMATION. Except as may be required in the performance of the work, Consultant agrees not to divulge any unpublished information, acquired as a Consultant to the Company from any source, including the Company, its customers and associate or other contractors, without the prior written consent of the Company.

10. TERMINATION. Either party may terminate this agreement in whole or in part at any time by giving written notice to the other.

IN WITNESS WHEREOF, the parties hereto have executed this agreement as of the day and year first above written.

CONSULTANT

By_____   _____

Date_____   Date_____

Appendix   C

Confidential Information Agreement

CONFIDENTIAL INFORMATION AGREEMENT

Agreement and acknowledgment, between <u>Your Company</u>, the undersigned, and <u>Your Client.</u>
The undersigned hereby agrees and acknowledges:

1. That while serving as Consultants to _____, certain trade secrets may become known to us. These trade secrets fall under the following descriptions:
    a)   Technical data: Methods, formulae, inventions, research material, designs, computer software, technical specifications, electronic systems, and security provisions.
    b)   Business data: Tactics, employee names, values, vulnerabilities, names of suppliers and subcontractors, operations, policies, and procedures.
2. While serving as Consultant or upon termination, we shall not make use of, or disclose or reveal to other parties, any confidential information or data aforementioned.
3. Hereby, in the event of termination of my Consulting relationship with the Company:
    a)   I will restore to the Company all documents relating to it, including: specifications, drawings, reports, manuals, blueprints, letters, software, marketing lists, and all other materials relating in any way to the Company's business, or issued by the Company while I was in its service. I also promise to return all copies of the aforementioned, except the copy permitted in the Contract. All retained computer disks shall be password-protected.
    b)   The Company reserves the right to inform any future or prospective employer or client of this agreement.
    c)   Any condition of this agreement which is held unenforceable, shall not affect any other condition.

_____   _____
Consultant's signature   Date

Appendix   D

Security Survey Work Sheets*

This is a basic guide that may be used to assist personnel in performing physical surveys in most industrial settings. Questions have been prepared for the purpose of reducing the possibility of neglecting to review certain areas of importance and to assist in the gathering of material for the survey.

GENERAL QUESTIONS BEFORE STARTING SURVEY

- Date of survey
- Interview with whom?
- Number of copies of survey desired by client; to be forwarded where?
- Obtain plot plan. Plot the production flow on plot plan and establish direction of north.
- Position and title of persons interviewed
- Correct name and address of plant
- Type of business or manufacture
- Square feet of production or manufacturing space
- Property other than main facility to be surveyed is located where?
- Property known as what?
- Property consists of what?
- What activity is in progress here?
- Is there other local property that will not be surveyed? Why?
- If plot plan is not complete, sketch remainder of property to be surveyed.

Number of Employees

- Administrative total number of all shifts.
- Skilled and unskilled—total number on each shift.

    1st shift
    2nd shift
    3rd shift
    Maintenance/cleanup crew

---

* From *Risk Analysis and the Security Survey*, by James F. Broader (Stoneham, MA: Butterworths, 1984).

Normal Shift Schedule and Break Times

- Salaried
- 1st Shift
- 2nd Shift
- 3rd Shift
- Maintenance/cleanup crew
- What days of the week is manufacturing in process?
- Are employees authorized to leave plant during breaks?
- Are hourly employees union or not?
- Are company guards in union bargaining unit?

Cafeteria

- Where is cafeteria located?
- What are hours of operation?
- Is it company or concession operated?
- What is security of proceeds from sales?
- What is security of foodstuffs?
- What is method of supply of foodstuffs?
- How are garbage and trash removed?
- Where is location of vending machines?
- Where is location of change-maker, if any?

Credit Union

- Where is credit union located?
- How is money secured?
- How are records secured?
- How is office secured?
- What are hours of operation?
- How much money is kept during day and overnight?

Custodial Service

- Is it outside contract or company employees?
- What hours do they actually start and complete work?
- Do they have keys in their possession?
- How is trash removed by them?
- Who, if anyone, controls removal?
- Who controls their entrance and exit?
- Are they supervised by any company employee?

Company Store

- Where is company store located?
- What are hours of operation?
- What is method used to control stock?
- How is stock supplied from plant?
- Number of clerks working in store?
- How is cash handled?
- When are inventories conducted, and who performs them?
- How are proceeds from sales secured?
- How is the store secured?

Petty Cash or Funds on Hand

- In what office are funds kept?
- What is the normal amount?
- How are these funds secured?
- What is the control and security of containers?
- Who has general knowledge of amount normally on hand?

Classified Operations

- Is government classified work performed?
- What is the degree of classification?
- How are classified documents secured?
- What is security during manufacture?
- What is classification of finished product?
- Are government cognizant officers on premises?
- Is company-classified R&D performed?
- Is company-classified work sensitive to industry?
- What degree of security is it given?
- What degree of security does it require?
- What are the locations of the various processing areas and containers?

Theft Experience

- Office machines or records
- Locker room incidents
- Pilferage of employees' autos
- Pilferage of vending machines
- Pilferage from money-changer
- Thefts of company-owned safety equipment

- Theft of tools
- Theft of raw material and finished product
- Are thefts systematic or casual?
- Have any definite patterns been established?
- Are background investigations conducted prior to employment of any personnel?
- What category of personnel are investigated?
- What is extent of investigations?

The foregoing questions, answered properly, will assist you in developing the degree of control required for various areas, which can be secured only through the interview—the more probing the interview the better. You should now also have a working knowledge of the general operational plan. Before starting your detailed examination and study, you must take a guided orientation tour of the facility to acquaint yourself with the physical setting. Make notes on your plot plan and pad during this tour.

I. PHYSICAL DESCRIPTION OF THE FACILITY

- Is the facility subject to natural disastrous phenomena?
- Describe in detail the above if applicable.
- What major vehicular and railroad arteries serve this facility?
- How many wood-frame buildings? Describe and identify them.
- How many load-bearing brick buildings? Describe and identify them.
- How many light or heavy steel-frame buildings? Describe and identify them.
- How many reinforced concrete buildings? Describe and identify them.
- Are all buildings within one perimeter? If not, describe.

II. PERIMETER SECURITY

- Describe type of fence, walls, buildings, and physical perimeter barriers.
- Is fencing of acceptable height, design, and construction?
- What is present condition of all fencing?
- Is material stored near fencing?
- Are poles or trees near fencing? If so, is height of fence increased?
- Are there any small buildings near fencing? If so, is the height of fence increased?
- Does undergrowth exist along the fencing?
- Is there an adequate clear zone on both sides along fencing?
- Can vehicles drive up to fencing?
- Are windows of buildings on the perimeter properly secured?
- Is wire mesh on windows adequate for its purpose?
- Are there any sidewalk elevators at this facility? If so, are they properly secured when not in operation?

- How are sidewalk elevators secured during operation?
- Do storm sewers or utility tunnels breach the barrier?
- Are these sewers or tunnels adequately secured?
- Is the perimeter barrier regularly maintained and inspected?
- How many gates and doors are there on the perimeter?
- Number used by personnel? (visitors, employees)
- Number used by vehicles?
- Number used by railroad?
- How is each gate controlled?
- Are all gates adequately secured and operating properly?
- Are railroad gates supervised by the guard force during operations?
- How are the railroad gates controlled?
- Do swinging gates close without leaving a gap?
- Are unused gates secured and sealed properly?
- What is security control of opened gates?
- Are chains and locks of adequate construction used to secure gates?
- Are any alarm devices used at the gates?
- Is CCTV used to observe gates or any part of the perimeter?
- How many doors from buildings open onto the perimeter?
- What type are they—personnel or vehicular?
- How are they secured when not in use?
- What is security control when in use?
- How many emergency doors breach the perimeter barrier?
- How are the emergency doors secured to prevent unauthorized use?
- Are there any unprotected areas on the perimeter?
- What portion of the fence do guards observe while making rounds?

III. BUILDING SECURITY

A.Offices

- Where are the various administrative offices located generally?
- When are offices locked?
- Who is responsible to check security at end of day?
- How and where are company records stored?
- How are they secured?
- Are vaults equipped with temperature thermostats (rate-of-rise; Pyro-Larm)?
- Are offices equipped with sprinklers? Fire extinguishers?
- Are any central station or local alarms installed to protect safes, cabinets, etc?
- Are various file cabinets locked?
- Are individual offices locked?
- Does the company have IBM computer rooms?
- What type of fire protection are they given?

B. Plant

- When and how are exterior doors locked?
- When and how are dock doors locked?
- Are individual plant offices locked?
- Are warehouses apart from production area secured?
- Are certain critical and vulnerable areas protected by alarms? What type?
- What are these areas? What do they contain?
- Are locker room windows covered by screening?

C. Tool Room

- Is one or more established?
- Departmental or central tool room?
- What is the method of control and receipt?
- How is tool room secured?

D. Locker Rooms

- What is basis of issue to individual?
- What is type of locker—wall or elevated basket type?
- How are individual lockers secured?
- Does company furnish keys/locks?
- Who or what department controls keys/locks?
- What control methods are used?
- How and when are keys and locks issued and returned?
- Are issued uniforms kept in lockers?
- Are unannounced locker inspections made?
- Who conducts inspections and how often?

Special Areas that May Require Additional Attention

If the facility houses the following types of activities, they may require special individual inspection. (Base recommendations on any or all of the applicable portions of the checklist.)

- Research and development areas
- Laboratories
- Storage areas for valuable, critical, or sensitive items
- Finished product test areas
- Finished product display areas
- Vehicle parking garages apart from the facility

- Vacant or used lofts, attics, etc.
- Mezzanines or sub-basements
- Aircraft hangars, maintenance shops, and crew quarters

Note: You will, after the initial inspection tour, design a checklist applicable to these special areas.

IV. SECURITY OF SHIPPING AND RECEIVING AREAS

- How many shipping docks, vehicle and railroad?
- What are the hours of operation of docks?
- What is the method of transportation?
- What is the method of inventory control at docks?
- What is the method of control of classified items?
- What is the security of classified or "hot" items?
- What supervision is exercised at the docks?
- Are loaded and unloaded trucks sealed?
- Who is responsible for sealing vehicles?
- What type of seals are being used?
- How are truck drivers controlled?
- Is there a designed waiting room for truck drivers?
- Is it separated from company employees?
- Are areas open to other than dock employees?
- Do guards presently supervise these areas? Is this necessary?
- What is the method of accounting for material received?
- Is shipping done by parcel post?
- What is the control at point of packaging?
- Who controls stamps or stamp machines?
- Who transports packages to post office?
- What is the method of transport to post office?
- Where is pick-up point at plant?
- What controls are exercised over the transport vehicle?
- Are inspections of operations made presently?
- Who conducts these inspections and how often?
- Does the facility have ship loading wharves or docks?
- Are contract longshoremen used?
- How do longshoremen get to and from the docks?
- If they pass through the facility, how are they controlled?
- How are ships' company personnel controlled when given liberty?
- Are any specific routes through the facility designated for longshoremen and ship personnel?
- If so, how is it marked and is it used?
- Are these personnel escorted?
- If they are not escorted, what measures are taken to escort them?
- Is there any way in which these personnel could be kept from passing through the facility?

V. AREA SECURITY

- Can guards observe outside areas from their patrol routes?
- Do guards expose themselves to attack?
- Are patrols staggered so no pattern is established?
- What products are stored in outside areas?
- Is parking allowed inside the perimeter?
- If so, are controls established and enforced?
- Where do employees, visitors, and officials park?
- What security and control is provided?
- Arc parking lots adequately secured?
- Is there a trash dump on the premises?
- How is it secured from the public?
- Is it operated by company employees?
- Is it approached directly from the manufacturing facility?
- Do roads within the perimeter present a traffic problem?
- Do rivers, canals, public thoroughfares, or railroads pass through the plant?
- Are loaded trucks left parked within the perimeter?
- If so, what protection is given them?
- Do the roads outside the facility present a traffic problem?
- What are these problems and how can they be remedied?
- Is there any recreational activity, such as baseball, within the perimeter?
- Are these areas fenced off from the remainder of the property?
- Could they logically be fenced off?

VI. PROTECTIVE LIGHTING

- Is protective lighting adequate on perimeter?
- What type of lighting is it?
- Is lighting of open areas within perimeter adequate?
- Do shadowed areas exist?
- Are outside storage areas adequately lighted?
- Arc inside areas adequately lighted?
- Is the guard protected or exposed by the lighting?
- Are gates adequately lighted?
- Do lights at gate illuminate interior of vehicles?
- Arc critical and vulnerable areas well illuminated?
- Is protective lighting operated manually or automatically?
- Do cones of light on perimeter overlap?
- Are perimeter lights wired in series?
- Is the lighting at shipping and receiving docks or piers adequate?
- Is lighting in the parking lots adequate?
- Is there an auxiliary power source available?
- Are the interiors of buildings adequately lighted?

- Are top secret and secret activities adequately lighted?
- Are guards equipped with powerful flashlights?
- How many more and what type of lights are needed to provide adequate illumination? In what locations?
- Do security personnel report light outages?
- How soon are burned out lights replaced?

VII. KEY CONTROL, LOCKING DEVICES, AND CONTAINERS

- Is there a grand-master, master, and submaster system? Describe it.
- Are locks used throughout the facility of the same manufacture?
- Is there a record of issuance of locks?
- Is there a record of issuance and inspection of keys?
- How many grand-master and master keys are there in existence?
- What is the security of grand-master and master keys?
- What is the security of the key cabinet or box?
- Who is charged with handling key control? Is the system adequate? Describe the control system.
- What is the frequency of record and key inspections?
- Are keys made at the plant?
- Do key gows have a special design?
- What is the type of lock used in the facility? Are all adequate in construction?
- Would keys be difficult to duplicate?
- Are locks changed periodically at critical locations?
- Are any "sesame" padlocks used for classified material storage areas or containers?
- If a key cutting machine is used, is it properly secured?
- Are key blanks adequately secured?
- Are investigations made when master keys are lost?
- Are locks immediately replaced when keys are lost?
- Do locks have interchangeable cores?
- Are extra cores properly safeguarded?
- Are combination locks three-position type?
- Are safes located where the guard can observe them on rounds?
- How many people possess combinations to safes and containers?
- How often are combinations changed?
- What type of security containers are used for the protection of: Money? Securities? High value metals? Company proprietary material? Government classified information?
- Are lazy-man combinations used?
- Are birth dates, marriage dates, etc., used as combinations?
- Are combinations recorded anywhere in the facility where they might be accessible to an intruder?

- Are the combinations recorded and properly secured so that authorized persons can get them in emergencies?
- Is the same or greater security afforded recorded combinations as that provided by the lock?
- Where government classified information is concerned, does each person in possession of a combination have the proper clearance and the "need to know"?
- Have all faces of the container locked with a combination lock been examined to see if combination is recorded?
- Are padlocks used on containers containing classified material chained to containers?

VIII. CONTROL OF PERSONNEL AND VEHICLES

- Are passes or badges used? By whom?
- Type used? Describe in detail?
- Is color coding used?
- Are badges uniformly worn on outer clothing?
- Are special passes issued? To whom? When?
- Who is responsible for issue and receipt of passes and badges?
- Are badges and passes in stock adequately secured?
- How are outside contractors controlled?
- How are visitors controlled?
- How are vendors controlled?
- How many employee entrances are there?
- What type of physical control is there at each entrance and exit?
- Where are the time clocks located?
- Is it possible to consolidate clock locations to one or two main clock alleys?
- Is there any control at time clock locations?
- Are there special entrances for people other than employees?
- How are the special entrances controlled?
- Are fire stairwells used for operational purposes?
- Does the facility use elevators to various floors?
- What control is exercised over their use?
- Are elevators used by operating employees?
- Do the elevators connect operational floors with strictly office floors?
- Does this present a problem in personnel control?
- Are the elevators automatic or attended?
- If automatic, are floor directories posted in them?
- Do avenues within the buildings used for emergency egress present a problem of personnel control?
- Examine pedestrian flow from entrance, to locker room, and to work area.

- Can changes be made to shorten routes or improve control of personnel in transit?
- Are personnel using unauthorized entrances and exits?
- If government classified work is being performed, are controls in use adequate to comply with the Defense Department pamphlet for safeguarding classified information?
- Are groups authorized to visit and observe operations?
- How are these groups controlled?
- Do registers used to register visitors, vendors, etc., contain adequate information?
- Are these registers regularly inspected? By whom?
- Are employees issued uniforms?
- Are different colors used for different departments?
- What control is exercised over employees during lunch and coffee breaks?
- Do guards or watch patrols ever accompany trash trucks or vending machine service personnel?
- Is parking authorized on premises within the perimeter?
- Are parking lots fenced off from the production areas?
- What method of control of personnel and vehicles is there from the parking lots?
- Is vehicle identification used?
- What types of vehicle stickers or identification are used?
- How are issue and receipt of stickers controlled?
- If executives park within the perimeter, are their autos exposed to employees?
- If nurses and doctors park within the perimeter, are their autos exposed to employees?
- Where do vendor service personnel park?
- Do vendor service personnel use plant vehicles to make the service tours? Are small vehicles available?
- How are outside contractor vehicles controlled?
- What method is used to control shipping and receiving trucks?
- Are the parking facilities adequate at the docks?
- Does parking present a problem in vehicle or personnel control?
- What is the problem encountered?
- During what hour does switching of railroad cars occur?
- Is it possible for persons to enter the premises during switching?
- Are there adequate directional signs to direct persons to specific activities?
- Are the various buildings and activities adequately marked to preclude persons from becoming lost?
- Are safety helmets required?
- Are safety shoes required?
- Are safety glasses required?
- Are safety gloves required?
- Are safety aprons required?
- Are full-time nurses or doctors available?
- Is there a vehicle available for emergency evacuation? What type is it?

IX. SAFETY FOR PERSONNEL

- How far away is the nearest hospital in time and distance?
- Are any company employees or guards trained in first aid?
- Is a safety director appointed?
- Is there a safety program? What does it consist of?
- How often does the safety committee meet?
- Is a first aid or medical room available?
- How are medicine cabinets secured?
- Who controls these keys?
- How is the first aid room secured?
- Are any narcotics on hand?
- If so, is there established narcotic security?
- Are the required safety equipment items worn? By visitors?
- What is the safety record of this facility?
- How does it compare with the national record?
- Are areas around machinery well policed?
- Does machinery have installed guards where needed? Are they used?
- Are mirrors used where needed to allow fork lift operators to observe "blind" turns?
- Could or would mechanical devices used for fork lift control improve safety?
- What type of device could be used? Pneumatic alarm system? Signal light?

X. ORGANIZATION FOR EMERGENCY

- Are doors adequate in number for speedy evacuation?
- Are they kept clear of obstructions and well marked?
- Are exit aisles clear of obstructions and well marked?
- Are emergency shutdown procedures developed and is the evacuation plan in writing?
- Do employees understand the plans?
- Are emergency evacuation drills conducted?
- Do guards have specific "emergency" duties? Do they know these duties?
- Are local police available to assist in emergencies?
- Are any areas of the building in this facility designated public C.D. shelters?
- If so, what control is established to isolate the area from the rest of the facility?
- Do the emergency plans provide for a designated repair crew? Is the crew adequately equipped and trained?
- Are shelters available and marked for use of employees?
- If the plant is subject to natural disastrous phenomena, what are they? Floods? Tornados?
- What emergency plans have been formulated to cope with these hazards?
- When and what was the latest incident of a natural disaster?
- Did it result in loss of life and/or loss of time?
- Attach a copy of the emergency procedures.

XI. THEFT CONTROL

- Are lunch-box inspections conducted?
- Is a package-pass control system being used? Describe it.
- Is a company-employed supervisor assigned to check the package-pass system regularly?
- Is a company official occasionally present during lunch-box inspections?
- Are package passes serially numbered or do they contain control numbers?
- Is security of package passes in stock adequate?
- Are comparison signatures available for the guards' comparison?
- Is the list of signatures kept up to date?
- What action is taken when anyone is caught stealing?
- What controls are established on tools loaned to employees?
- What controls are established on laundry being removed?
- What is the method of removal of scrap and salvage?
- What controls are exercised over removal of useable scrap?
- Is control of this removal adequate?
- Are vending and service vehicle inspections being conducted?
- Do employees carry lunch boxes to their work areas?
- Are railroad cars inspected entering and leaving the plant?
- Are company-owned delivery or passenger vehicles authorized to park inside buildings of the plant?
- Does this parking constitute a possible theft problem?
- Do guards check outside the perimeter area for property thrown over fences?
- Do guards occasionally inspect trash pick-up? Does anyone?

XII. SECURITY GUARD FORCES

- What is present guard coverage—hours per day and total hours per week?
- Describe in detail guard organization and composition.
- Number and times of shifts each 24-hour period during weekdays and weekends?
- Number of stationary posts? When are they staffed?
- Number of patrol routes? When and where are they and when are patrols made?
- Are tours supervised by ADT or DETEX stations or both?
- How many stations? Locate them on your plot plan. (Use different colors or shapes or symbols for different floors and routes.)
- What is length of time of each patrol?
- Is there additional coverage on Saturday, Sunday, or holidays?
- Do the patrol routes furnish adequate protection as presently established?
- Are the guards required to be deputized?
- Are armed guards required?
- How do guards communicate while on patrol?

- Are written guard instructions available? If so, secure a copy.
- If no written instructions are available, generally describe duties of each shift and post.
- What equipment does the guard force have issued? Need?
- Do they require security clearances? What degree?
- Do they require special training?
- Is there a training program in force?
- What communications are available to the guard force to call outside the facility?
- Is the number of guards, posts, and patrol routes adequate?
- Are mechanical or electrical devices used in conjunction with the guard force?
- Do the guards know how to operate, reset, and monitor the devices properly?
- Do the guards know how to respond when the alarms are activated?
- Are guards included in emergency plans?
- Do guards know their duties? Emergency duties?
- Do guards make written reports of incidents?
- Are adequate records of incidents maintained?
- Are the guards familiar with the use of fire-fighting equipment?

Recommendations for changes must indicate each post, patrol, and so forth by number of hours for weekdays, weekends, and holidays, and brief description of the guard's duties. List the total present coverage, total after recommendations, and the differences in hours. If your recommendations increase coverage you should justify the hours and the cost.

Appendix   E

Security Checklist

David L. Berger

Forensic Consultant, Security Law Enforcement
11600 Montana Avenue, Los Angeles, CA 90049
Tel. (310) 826 7386

Many clients have requested that I assist in the preparation of depositions and interrogatories. For that purpose I have prepared the following checklist of information, relating to security, that should be obtained in order that I may arrive at a comprehensive analysis and prepare a presentable presentation for trial.

The list contains a great deal of information which may not be relevant in this instance, thus I have checked those sections which relate directly to this case.

STATISTICAL DATA

- Area "Part One" crime statistics from the local law enforcement agencies reporting district where the incident occurred. Also adjacent reporting districts for comparison and analysis. Please obtain reports for a three year period prior to the date of this occurrence. This information usually must be obtained by *Subpoena Duces Tecum.*
- Obtain records or documentation of all crimes committed on the premises where the incident occurred. Incident reports, logs and follow-up investigation from the security department or management office. Obtain three years.
- Search the Superior and/or Municipal court index to ascertain whether there have been any prior court actions of a similar nature.
- Compare, through either physical inspection or statistical data, the crime rates and/or physical security between the location of the incident and other similar locations in the immediate vicinity.

PHYSICAL SECURITY

- Does the location utilize closed circuit television?
- How many cameras and their locations?

154

- How many monitors and their locations?
- What type cameras are installed?
- Lenses?
- Horizontal line resolution?
- Are the cameras monitored?
- By whom?
- What hours?
- Video tape?
- Motion alarm?
- Does the location utilize two-way radio communication?
- What power (watts) for base station and walkie-talkies?
- What frequency band?
- Does the location utilize intercom systems?
- Does the location utilize "beeper" or paper systems?
- Does the location maintain alarm systems?
  - Fire?
  - Holdup?
  - Burglar?
  - Other?
- Are the alarms an in-house system?
- Are the alarms maintained by an alarm company? Identify the company.
- Are the alarms silent or audible?
- Are there any "panic bar," alarmed exit doors?
- Identify all doors and windows which are physically "wired" to the alarm system.
- Identify all "motion detection" units incorporated into the alarm system (ultra sonic, radar, laser, light beams, etc.).
- How frequently (and by whom) is the alarm system tested?
- Identify all personnel who are on the alarm company's emergency call list.
- Has this facility ever been cited or fined or in any manner been advised of excessive "false alarms."
- Does the location employ computerized or electronic access control systems? If so, describe and identify.
- Is there a safe or vault at the location?
- Describe the types of locks employed on all interior and exterior doors.
- Spring lock or deadbolt?
- Manufacturer and model number of lock?
- Length of deadbolt?
- What material is door constructed of?
- What material is door frame constructed of?
  - Wood?
  - Metal?
- What other types of bolts, latches or chains are utilized?
- Are padlocks used on doors or gates?
- Do locks require keys or combinations?

- If a "card-key" system is utilized, identify.
- Is a commercial "key control" system maintained on the premises?
- Where is the key cabinet located?
- Who has access to the key control cabinet?
- Who is in charge of issuing keys?
- How often and by whom is a key inventory conducted?
- Do persons have to sign for keys when issued?
- Is a record kept of lost or stolen keys?
- Are lock keyways interchangeable on all doors?
- Are door locks changed when a key is reported stolen or missing?
- Are locks changed on a regular basis?
- How frequently and by whom are locks serviced?
- Do any doors have "peepholes" or other viewing devices for the purpose of identifying the caller?
- If *no* commercial key control system is utilized, identify the employee who is responsible for issuing keys or other access control devices. If no particular employee is authorized, then what department handles keys?
- Are any "anti-shim" bars or devices utilized on doors?
- Does one "grand-master" key open all doors or is the system broken down to "submasters." If a "submaster" system is utilized, describe the pattern?
- Identify personnel carrying master keys at any level.
- Are grand-master or master keys permitted off the premises or are they turned in each evening or at the end of each shift?
- How are windows secured?
  - Locks?
  - Bolts?
  - Latches?
- Are rods, bars or other devices utilized in the tracks of sliding glass windows?
- How are sliding glass doors secured?
  - Locks?
  - Bolts?
  - Latches?
- Are rods, bars or other devices utilized in the tracks of sliding glass doors?
- Are exterior windows protected by bars. If so, are they the "solid" or "breakaway" type for emergency exit?
- If the building is a multi-story structure, are the stairwell doors equipped with locks?
- Are they kept unlocked at all times?
- Do the stairwell doors lock from inside the stairwell?
- Is the ground floor exit door alarmed or equipped with an emergency exit panic bar?
- Are restroom doors locked or unlocked at all times?
- Do elevators require a key to operate?
- Do elevators operate automatically or do they require an operator?

- Is there an elevator panel indicating the location of each cab? Where is the panel located?
- Are the elevators turned off at any time of the day or night after closing?
- Are there any special security floors to which the elevator will not respond?
- Are there separate elevators which descend to an underground parking level only?
- Are elevator cabs equipped with emergency telephones?
- Is exterior or perimeter fencing utilized?
- How high is fence?
- What gauge wire is the fence constructed of?
- If not "wire" of what is the fence constructed?
- Is the fence equipped with barbed wire or razor ribbon?
- Does the fence utilize sensor, or other, alarm devices? Is the fence posted with warning signs?
- How are the fence gates secured?
  - Locks?
  - Padlocks?
- Is interior fencing utilized? If so, identify and describe as above exterior fencing
- Is there an exterior parking lot or parking structure?
- How many vehicle capacity?
- How many floors to the structure?
- Is the structure above ground level?
- Is the structure below ground level?
- Is the parking area equipped with closed circuit television?
- Is the parking area patrolled by security guards or other employees?
- Patrolled on foot?
- Patrolled utilizing a vehicle?
- What is the frequency of patrols?
- Are employees, guests or other persons escorted to their vehicles after dark? By whom?
- Is the parking area well lighted? Describe.
- Is the parking area properly posted with signs indicating that the property is "private" and that unauthorized vehicles or persons will not be permitted, etc.?
- Do parking areas have separate sections for visitors, guests, employees, etc.?
- Is the parking area attended?
- Company employee?
- Leased to parking company?
- Security officer?
- Is there a charge for parking?
- Does the parking attendant work from a booth or other structure?
- Does the structure maintain communication with the main building through a telephone, two-way radio or intercom?
- Is the parking attendant's booth equipped with a holdup alarm?
- Does the parking attendant handle cash?
- Where is the cash kept?

- Is cash transported to either the main building or any other location after any given amount is accumulated?
- In what manner is the cash transported?
- What type of exterior lighting is utilized?
- Tungsten, mercury or carbon vapor, etc.?
- Approximate wattage of each light?
- Are lights equipped with tamper proof housings or anti-vandal screens?
- How many lights are installed and where are they located?
- How frequently are lights checked to see if they are operational or burned out? When are burned out lights replaced?
- Are the exterior lights connected to an emergency generator or battery pack in case of power failure?
- What lighting is utilized in the common areas of the building? Describe wattage, locations, etc.
- Are there any emergency lights installed on the exterior, in interior halls, stairwells, etc. which are designed to be turned on in case of a general power failure to the structure? Where located?
- What, if any, lights are left on after closing?

ACCESS CONTROL

- Do employees or guests have to sign in and/or show identification prior to entering either day or night?
- Who signs in persons entering the building?
- If sign-in logs are maintained, obtain copies for the day of the incident and as far back as relevant to this issue.
- Is the property posted "private property" with the appropriate "trespassing" notification?
- What are the requirements to gain entry to the premises?

GUARD SERVICE

- Does the location of the occurrence employ security guards?
- In house guards?
- Contract security guard service?
- Patrol service?
- Does the location employ a Director of Security?
- Identify the Director.
- Provide a copy of the Directors resume or employment application.
- If no Director of Security, who is responsible for maintaining security at the location?
- How many guards are assigned to each shift?
- Uniformed?

- Plainclothes?
- Is there a guard supervisor for each shift?
- Security Director?
- Assistant Director of Security?
- Captain?
- Lieutenant?
- Sergeant Senior Security Officer?
- Other?
- Provide the names of all guards who were on duty at the time of the occurrence. Provide also their employment applications and/or resume of experience.
- If "In-house" guards?
- Are the guards required to possess certification from the State of California that they passed the required "Powers to Arrest" course (guard cards)?
- Are the guards armed with:
  - Firearms?
  - Baton (straight or PR-24)?
  - Chemical agents (tear gas—Macc)?
- If armed, do they possess certification by the State of California indicating that they took and passed the proper courses and possess valid authorization to carry said weapons?
- Are the guards trained in first aid?
- Are the guards trained in fire control and prevention?
- Are the guards trained in the legal aspects of apprehensions and detention?
- What other training is provided to the guards?
- Who is responsible for training the security force?

If contract guards:

- Who in the company supervises the guards?
- Are the guards' credentials checked by anyone in the company prior to allowing them to assume a post?
- Does the contract service provide supervision?
- On-site supervision?
- Roving supervisors?
- Provide a copy of the contract with the contract guard service.
- Is the contract guard service licensed by the State of California? If so, provide the license number.
- Is the contract guard service maintaining liability insurance or bonding?
- Provide identification regarding the insurance company, policy number, limits of liability, etc.
- Provide information regarding the bonding.
- Did any member of the guard company staff survey the company and make recommendations regarding security coverage?
- List those recommendations.
- Were the recommendations followed?
- Describe the guards' uniforms.
  - Badges?

- Sleeve patches?
- Color of shirt and trousers?
- Hats?
- Do guards carry a Detex clock or any other device designed to indicate guards' location and/or time arrived at any given location?
- Do guards patrol the premises?
- Indicate patrol routes. Provide times of patrols.
- Specific duties during patrols.
- Do guards stand (or sit) at stationary posts?
- Identify post locations.
- What are guards' duties at said posts?
- Do guards drive patrol vehicles?
- Are the patrol vehicles marked, identifying them as "security"?
- Do the vehicles have special lights or flashing beacons?
- Are the vehicles equipped with two-way radios?
- Are guards required to maintain daily activity logs?
- Obtain copies of the logs during the day of the incident and for one week prior.
- Are the guards required to write reports or fill out specific incident report forms?
- Obtain copies of reports relating to the specific incident in question.
- Obtain copies of all reports dealing with similar incidents over a period of three years.
- Does the security department, or any other department of the company, file reports and logs and/or maintain an index file of said reports?
- Who reviews the above logs and reports?
- Are any statistics derived from the above logs and reports and are those statistics used in revising guard and patrol activities or investigative procedures?
- What is the guards' rate of pay beginning with the entry level salary?
- What does the company pay, per hour, to the contract guard service?
- What salary do the contract guards receive by the hour?
- What procedures are used to check guards' applications (i.e. check former employer, education, training, etc.)?

MISCELLANEOUS

- Are employees, guests, tenants or visitors notified, in any way (written or orally) of any "crime problems" or other existing dangerous circumstances which may pose a threat to their safety?
- If the answer is "yes," obtain copies of any notices or identify the individual who orally provided the warning.
- Are any printed notices or bulletins issued on a regular or occasional basis regarding suggestions on security measures or how an individual may help in protecting himself or his property?

- Are any warning signs posted throughout the property, designed to act as a deterrence to criminal activity?
- Does the company offer a "reward" for the apprehension and conviction of criminals or for information leading to their arrest and conviction?
- Has the company or property ever retained a professional "Security Consultant" or other knowledgeable security professional for the purpose of designing or reviewing the security system and/or program? Identify.
- Has the company or property ever consulted the local law enforcement agency for advice on security matters?
- Have any company management, or other personnel, who have responsibilities within the security function, had any formal training in "security" or "law enforcement" procedures?

- _____
- _____
- _____
- _____
- _____
- _____

Appendix   F

Consultant's Timeslip

CLIENT

ACTIVITY [   ] _____

DESCRIPTION _____

RE: _____

DATE _____ TIME START _____ TIME STOP _____

TIME SPENT _____ BILLABLE [   ]   N/C [   ]

ENTERED DATE _____

ACTIVITY [   ] _____

DESCRIPTION

_____

_____

_____

RE: _____

DATE _____ TIME START _____ TIME STOP _____

TIME SPENT _____ BILLABLE [   ]   N/C [   ]

ENTERED DATE _____

1 office   2 on-site   3 travel time   4 research   5 phone   6 meeting

EXPENSES   CLIENT NAME _____

DATE   TYPE   DETAIL   AMOUNT   ENTERED

7   Parking   8   Airfare   9   Exp. Shipping   10   Mileage   11   Car rental

12 Gasoline   13 Food   14 Lodging

Bibliography

Broder, James F. *Risk Analysis and the Security Survey*. Boston: Butterworth, 1984.

Chronicle Guidance Publications. *Security Consultants* (brief 563). Moravia, NY: Chronicle Guidance Pub., Inc., 1987.

Connor, Richard A., Jr., and Jeffrey P. Davidson. *Marketing Your Consulting and Professional Services*. New York: John Wiley & Sons, 1985.

Crawford, Mary Alice. "Consultants on Consultants." *Security Management* (February 1984): 16.

Holtz, Herman. *How to Succeed as an Independent Consultant*. New York: John Wiley & Sons, 1983.

Janson, John J., Jr. "Security Consultant?" *Professional Protection* (March/April 1983): 36.

Janson, John J., Jr. "Time: What is Yours Worth?" *Professional Protection* (March 1982): 10.

Kaufer, Steve, CPP. "A User's Guide to Consultants." *Security Management* (February 1991).

Kaufer, Steve, CPP. "Using Outside Expertise to Improve Security." *Security Technology and Design Magazine* (March 1995).

Keller, Stephen R., CCP. "Clearing Up Cloudy Skies." *Security Management* (January 1988): 47.

Littlejohn, Robert F., CPP. *Consulting: A New Role for the Security Manager*, Encyclopedia of Security Management. Boston: Butterworth-Heinemann, 1993.

Lydon, Kerry. "Stretching Dollars with Consulting Services." *Security* (February 1988). 57.

National Forensic Center. *The Expert and the Law*. A Publication of the National Forensic Center, vol. 8 no.3 (1988): 4.

Poynter, Dan. *The Expert Witness Handbook*. Santa Barbara, CA: Para Publishing, 1987.

Serb, Tom. "Calling All Consultants." *Security World* (January 1983): 9.

Shenson, Howard L., and Jerry R. Wilson. *138 Quick Ideas to Get More Clients*. New York: John Wiley & Sons, 1993.

Siver, Edward W. "The Ten Commandments for Choosing and Using Consultants." *Risk Management* (June 1983): 64.

"So You Want To Be a Consultant." *Security Management* (February 1991).

Veich, A.M. "Guidelines for Garnering a Good Consultant." *Security Management* (January 1992).

Walsh, Timothy J., and Richard J. Healy. *The Protection of Assets Manual*. Santa Monica, CA: The Merritt Company, 1985.

Index